Thoughts on *You Are C...*
Whether You Lik...

"I've read this book twice now, and here's what I can tell you: it's the kind of book that you'll want to keep and reread because it rings so true and touches you so deeply."
— Brian McLaren, author of *Faith After Doubt*

David LaMotte's book, *You Are Changing The World*, is beautifully and sincerely written from the perspective of an artist in the movement for love and justice LaMotte captures the rhythm and artistry that exist in efforts to change the world for the better.
— Bishop William J. Barber, II, President, Repairers of the Breach, Co-chair, Poor People's Campaign: A National Call for Moral Revival

The need for the wisdom, courage, and solid advice that I find in this book was the very reason I founded the Center over 35 years ago. David LaMotte is a very good partner in this important work, both for our world and for the human soul.
— Richard Rohr, *Center for Action and Contemplation*

"This book serves as an antidote to the hopelessness so many of us feel about our world today. LaMotte demonstrates that hope is not naive optimism, but a determination to help build a better world. Through his many examples of communities of ordinary people who are demonstrating that disparate people with differing opinions can live in harmony, LaMotte encourages us to find our own way out of cynicism and despair."
— Kathleen Norris, author of *Embracing a Life of Meaning*

David brings his gifts of experience as an artist, songwriter, all around creative and experienced activist into a work that is much more than a manual for world-changers. This book is pure gift. A pure gift of [en]couragement. It infuses you with the courage to first be that new world we are laboring to manifest.
— Anthony Smith, co-founder, Transform Network

David LaMotte is a gifted storyteller. Through stories of his own lived experience in spaces across the world, he reminds us to keep re-imagining the ways that we as faith leaders, activists, organizers, artists and other change agents do the work to which we are called. I look forward to using this book in my own work for equity and justice.
— Tami Forte Logan, founding director of *Faith 4 Justice Asheville*

As one of my closest friends, David LaMotte has helped me with a thousand things. But in this book, he can help all of us rethink our misconceptions about how change happens, and the role each of us can play in it. Miracles happen, but they may not be spectacular or attention-grabbing. Instead, the work of contributing to the common good while avoiding both burnout and egocentrism moves bit by bit, with you and me woven into a tapestry of actions, thoughts, words, ideas, prayers and stories. You are already changing the world by your very presence - this book will help you gain more clarity about how to do it better, and love yourself - and life - more.
— Gareth Higgins, author of *How Not to Be Afraid*

You Are Changing the World is an unselfish offering of wisdom, personal transparency, and deep thoughtfulness. As I move through the ebbs and flows of changing the world with what is mine to do, I'll keep this book close by.
— Yara T. Allen, Director of Theomusicology and Cultural Arts, Repairers of the Breach

In this era of climate chaos, white supremacist violence, global pandemics, hyper-polarized political discourse, and threatened nuclear annihilation, there is a pervasive sense of powerlessness. In this book, David LaMotte provides us inspiring examples of the possible and the practical to reconnect us with our human family, this fragile earth, and a hope-centered way of life. A nonviolent practitioner of "Good Trouble," LaMotte shows that we have all the tools we need to create Beloved Community in our time.

— Ethan Vesely-Flad, Director of National Organizing, Fellowship of Reconciliation

David LaMotte has created a powerful antidote to the helplessness we often feel in a world that is overwhelming in both its pain and its beauty. With seriously good cheer, he helps us think about how to engage this world with courage, grace, and hope, in the ways that are distinctly ours to do. I am especially grateful for his stories and his wisdom that remind us that as we do this, we are not alone.

— Jan Richardson, author of *The Cure for Sorrow*

YOU ARE
CHANGING
THE WORLD

Whether You Like it or Not

David LaMotte

chalice
PRESS

Copyright © 2023 by David LaMotte

All rights reserved. For permission to reuse content, please contact Copyright Clearance Center, 222 Rosewood Drive, Danvers, MA 01923, (978) 750-8400, www.copyright.com.

Print 9780827208544

EPUB 9780827208551

EPDF 9780827208568

ChalicePress.com

Printed in the United States of America

For Deanna and Mason,

*who have changed my world
and enriched my life
more than I could have imagined.*

You are my home.

Contents

Acknowledgments

I have been working on writing this book for several years now and, as with all good efforts to have a positive impact, there have been many people involved who need to be thanked. I'm sure I will remember to list only some of them here, but I hope that friends whom I omit will understand my gratitude through other means.

In 2021, I was moved and elated to find myself in conversation with Chalice Press about revising, expanding, updating, and republishing this book, which was originally published as *Worldchanging 101: Challenging the Myth of Powerlessness*. Big thanks to Brad Lyons, David Woodard, and all the crew there for seeing the importance of the conversation this book is trying to advance, and for welcoming me to the Chalice team. And deep gratitude to Deborah Arca for first suggesting that Chalice might be a good fit for the book.

My wife, Deanna, is a wise voice in my life and my favorite editor, as well as being my true love, and I'm grateful to her for making me finish the book in the first place (pursuant to a rule she established for me: I can't start the next big project until I finish the current one) and for pushing me out the door to finish this new edition. I'm so deeply grateful to her for believing in the value of this effort and actively making space for it, not to mention for marrying me and braiding her story with mine.

Ulrike Guthrie edited this book with skill, wisdom, kindness, and generous tolerance for my occasional insistence on grammatical unorthodoxy in the service of accessibility. Ginna Bairby edited the first iteration of this book and helped me develop these ideas and the best words with which to express them.

Caroline and Allen Proctor, David Sardinha, Marty Mulligan, my parents John and Olivia LaMotte, and my sister and brother-in-law Margaret and Lee Torrence all welcomed me into physical spaces for me to take writing retreats. I could not be more grateful. Also, the staff of the Horry County Library in Surfside Beach, South Carolina, gave me room to work on this new edition, and they were wonderfully helpful in finding sources.

I am so grateful to the team of folks who keep my life and work up and running every day—Ernie Gregg, Jess Fox, Steve Roach-Knight, and Jen Thorstad. Also a big thanks to Kara, Barbie, MJ, Heather, Kathy, and to all the other good folks who have worked with me over the years.

First readers for the book include some family, some close friends, and some people with deep life experience in the work of changing the world (often in overlapping categories). Deep gratitude to Dennis Smith, Mindy Maddux, Liz Frencham, Hugh Hollowell, Rob Stephens, Will Nash, Jamie and Gwyn Ridenhour, Dr. Diane Johnson, Yara Allen, and my wife, Deanna LaMotte, my sister Kathy LaMotte, and my parents John and Olivia LaMotte. Margaret Aymer Oget and Deb Fox helped me to think through some thorny questions of wording and wisdom, and Brian O'Connors, Maryl Neff, Wade Burns, Ed Loring, Patrick Miller, Susan and George Reed, and David Gill helped me to clarify some fuzzy memories. Thanks to Pat Shufeldt for research assistance. Eric Bannan not only gave me great feedback on the original publication of the book but also named an album after one of the chapter titles, *Stumbling Toward the Light*. Thanks to Aleta McClenney for the photo of Mason's protest sign, and to Sarah Rudisill for creating graphics for this book.

One of the main themes of this book is discernment, trying to perceive the path in front of us. I am deeply grateful to Friends at Swannanoa Valley Friends Meeting for providing the space to listen for leading and for deep, sustaining friendship. I look to my faith community to challenge me and nourish me in equal measure, and I find both gifts there.

Sincere thanks to friends at the Montreat Conference Center, where I have encountered so many people and experiences that I treasure. Thanks for continuing to invite me back after all these years and for serving the world in all the ways that you do.

Special thanks as well to Rotary International and the Rotary Foundation for selecting me as a Rotary Peace Fellow. That opportunity and experience have opened doors and enriched my life in ways that I could never have imagined, and I am grateful to you for believing in my capacity to change the world, as well as for the changes you are effecting yourselves.

Most of the costs of the initial printing of this book were covered thanks to the generosity of 357 folks who contributed to a Kickstarter campaign. Without that initial printing, I would not have found my way to Chalice, and I am deeply grateful to everyone who helped birth this book by joining that effort. I love the fact that the funding for this book mirrors one of its messages—that through the accumulation of many efforts, small and large, we can do so much more than we can do on our own. I am profoundly grateful to the kind folks in my Patreon community (patreon.com/davidlamotte), who sustain me and provide treasured friendship, encouragement, and accountability.

Last, and most important of all, thanks to *you* for reading this book. Doing so is an indication that you care; you know that your world has a population of more than one. Human beings make the most sense in community, and community can only be created by risking, by reaching past the places where we are comfortable. I hope this book will encourage and challenge you, in equal measure. Regardless of how you intersect with it, though, thank you for being the kind of person who would choose to read such a book. Blessings on your efforts to change the world for the better.

So what do you need now?

That's what this book offers.

First, a growing activist like you needs understanding... understanding of what activism is, understanding of the differences between anger and hate, or hope and optimism, or fixing the world and changing it, or the Hero Narrative and the Movement Narrative. You need understanding about how movements grow and change happens in a complicated world.

Second, a growing activist like you needs encouragement, encouragement to keep going when progress seems slow or nonexistent, encouragement to keep learning, encouragement to take care of yourself as you care for others, encouragement to work in solidarity and community with others.

Third, you need stories, concrete stories of real people who have helped catalyze needed change against seemingly insurmountable obstacles. Those stories—some of them of people you already know, like Rosa Parks, Nelson Mandela, and John Lewis, and some of them of people you'll learn about here for the first time—will help you face your obstacles differently.

Fourth, you need concrete steps... simple, practical guidance. You need guidance about starting small, about acknowledging your own limitations and imperfections, and about avoiding predictable dangers and dead ends.

Fifth, as a growing activist, you need balance, because often we make one mistake and then react against it by making an opposite mistake. Seasoned, balanced wisdom can help you avoid both the dangers on one side and the opposite dangers on the other.

Sixth and finally, you need focus. You can't do everything. So you'll need to discern, "What is mine to do?" That clarity of focus will free you to celebrate the good work others are doing in their own areas of focus as you pursue what is yours to do.

Understanding, encouragement, stories, steps, balance, and focus: these are six of the great treasures you will find in this book.

I know, because I found them here myself.

I've read this book twice now, and here's what I can tell you: it's the kind of book that you'll want to keep and reread because it rings so true and touches you so deeply.

This hot-mess world needs changing, and there are beautiful, unique contributions that only you can make. Your life will be so much more full and meaningful for making them, and this book can be your guide and companion.

—Brian McLaren

Preface (2022)

I began writing an earlier edition of this book in 2009, and worked on it fairly steadily for the next five years while living in Australia, India, and the United States. It was originally published in 2014. It is reasonable to ask why Chalice Press and I have decided to make the investment to update, expand, and re-publish it, eight years after the original printing.

In the years since that first printing, the world has groaned and shifted under the weight of history and current events, and I have watched and participated as the ideas with which I wrestle here played out in front of me. Some of them have continued to grow and shift. Experience and conversation with friends and mentors have continued to add nuance. I have seen the work of activism done very well—and very poorly.

In addition to movements for positive change, we have seen the strengthening and mainstreaming of movements for White supremacy, marching through Charlottesville with their infamous tiki torches and polo shirts, and successfully working to elect politicians with open ties to their movements. In the first edition of this book, I largely focused on movements for positive change. In this one, I have added a chapter on toxic movements and 'astroturf,' the practice of manufacturing fake grass roots movements to influence political decisions or public opinion.

Since its original publication, the book that has become this one was used as a textbook for college classes at universities across the United States and Australia and has been read by many thousands of people. I have received many letters and emails over those years, including some quite recently, that convince me that the ideas shared here are still relevant and needed in the public discourse. I am thrilled that the folks at Chalice agree and that this conversation may broaden with the publication of this new edition.

This new iteration also gives more attention to personal sustainability, with more focus on discerning what is *not* ours to do than the original. Burnout seems to be on the rise among teachers, preachers, and activists, and it is an essential conversation to have.

My friend, Ron Davis, is a builder. He tells me what any contractor or carpenter will tell you: lumber is not what it used to be. Not only are two-by-fours not actually two-by-fours anymore (the standard for many years has been 3 ½ by 1 ½", and now they are getting thinner than that), the wood itself is also not as strong.

There are a few reasons for this. One is that modern forestry prioritizes trees that grow faster, rather than stronger, so they can get the lumber to market more quickly. According to Ron, a standard yellow pine used to grow for twelve to fifteen years before being harvested. Now it's about seven.

These days, tree farms also plant trees in straight rows, so they are easier to harvest, but there may be a downside to planting them that way. The wind can sail down those aisles between the trees, and the trees don't have to bend and sway nearly as much as they did in old growth forests. Resistance to that wind is part of what makes trees stronger, just as repeatedly picking up a heavy weight develops human muscles. As Lee Reich writes in Fine Gardening magazine, "Movement of the trunk helps strengthen it by thickening it and giving it taper from bottom to top. Trunk movement also stimulates root growth."

The same could be said of the ideas in this book. The first time I wrote this book, it took me about five years. Then I published it. After I had been in intimate relationship with these words and the ideas they represent for five years, they were finally fixed and static; and my relationship with those words, or at least that phase of it, was abruptly over. Meanwhile, a few thousand other people began to have their own relationships to the book and make their own connections, sometimes resonating and sometimes pushing back. I wasn't there. The dialog happened with the book itself. Now I have the opportunity to rejoin the conversation.

In the intervening years, a few things have happened, as you have probably noticed. Parts of the Obama and Biden presidencies, and the entirety of the Trump years fall within that time. George Floyd's murder and the ongoing racial reckoning it precipitated, the Black Lives Matter movement, a global pandemic, the Me Too movement, the Poor People's Campaign, the Women's March, wars, shootings, and terrorism, the gutting of Roe v. Wade, and a great deal of grassroots activism, working for both noble and troubling ends. All of those events have had a bearing on this book. These world events are wind, continuing to challenge, shape and strengthen these ideas and narratives.

I hope the lessons that my life has taught me intersect meaningfully with the lessons that your life has taught you. Different lives teach different lessons, and I treasure the exchange.

degree. The organization is run by the descendants of a legendary Gandhian activist who went by the name of Gora. Most of his nine children remain actively involved in social justice and sustainable development work, and the next generation contains some impressive peace and justice workers as well.

It is an extraordinary opportunity for me.

My experience in India so far has been gritty, intense, and discouraging while at the same time overflowing with kindness, warmth, and hope. Those things are not mutually exclusive. They may be mixed together in a single day as inextricably as water buffalo milk in chai.

My wife, our one-year-old son, and I bathe with a small bucket and a mug, and we use the same bucket to wash our clothes. We have learned to eat with our hands; by now it's somewhat natural and reasonably effective. Toilet paper is not common here. These things are not really hardships; they are how the vast majority of the world lives. Still, they are unfamiliar to us and serve as daily reminders of our usual privilege, and of the fact that there are many different definitions of 'normal.'

They are also reminders of the personal cost of middle-class material comfort and its tendency to distance us from our own surroundings. In India, Haiti, Guatemala, and other "developing countries" in which I've been fortunate enough to eat and sleep from time to time, I find that death seems a little closer. It is not kept out of sight so that we can deny its reality; it is a present possibility in each new day (certainly any day that involves driving in Indian traffic!).

The beautiful and surprising corollary is that *life* seems closer as well. The colors are somehow more vivid, the tastes richer on my tongue, the relationships and casual interactions less disposable.

Last Sunday afternoon, I spent a few hours talking with Lavanam, the second oldest of the Gora children. Eighty years old as of this writing, Lavanam is still politically active on various issues, including the ongoing negotiations between the Indian government and the Naxalite Maoist rebels in the hills nearby. He has been in dialogue with the rebels in recent years, arguing for the value of nonviolence as a tool in their often-violent revolutionary struggle; at the same time, he's been meeting with the government regarding the legitimacy of the rebels' concerns about the marginalization of the rural poor. Though he has written many books, Lavanam is no ivory tower academic, distant from the gritty realities of conflict and poverty.

Lavanam also told me stories of his teenage years and conversations he had with Gandhi while living on his ashram, as well as his many decades of passionate engagement since then. As we talked, he articulated one of his central concerns about development work: that most international development work seems to be based on a Western model and is, therefore, "opportunity-based."

Creating opportunities is not a bad thing. But Lavanam argues that opportunity-based development can be destructive to a community because it appeals primarily to individualist and materialist motivations. What is needed, he suggests, is *value*-based development, which does not ask how an individual may better his or her lot, but rather asks how individuals may contribute to the betterment of their communities.

> Value-based development... does not ask how an individual may better his or her lot, but rather asks how individuals may contribute to the betterment of their communities.

I am still early in my time here, and I know there are many stories to come. I love good stories, whether I'm the one listening to them or telling them, and that may be why I have been invited to speak to various groups in recent years about some of my experiences.

In those talks, I often frame my thoughts around ideas of how we as individuals can have a positive impact on the world around us, what could be called 'practical idealism.' Most people on the planet have much more potential to make an impact than we imagine. For most of us, the main thing standing in the way of making that impact is a belief in limitations that don't actually exist.

While I am unashamedly interested in motivating people, my talks bear little resemblance to what most people think of as "motivational speaking"—that is, motivating people for personal gain and enrichment. That holds little interest or appeal for me. I am much more interested in motivating people to have a positive impact on their larger social contexts, not just on their individual material situations. That serves everyone better, as research shows.

In their book *The Dragonfly Effect*, Andy Smith and Jennifer Lynn Aaker cite a sociological study that examined both people's perceptions of what makes them happy and what *really* does. They found that people tend to believe that material gain, affluence, and leisure will make them happy (a job promotion, a new car, a trip to the Bahamas, etc.).

When they interviewed people who consider themselves happy, however, those factors were not significantly correlated. Rather, they found that the common denominator among people who really *are* happy is a sense that their lives have meaning. That they matter. That they are of service.

That rings true to me, and it is one reason I've written this book. At its core, this book is about practical ways to live a life that matters and about some of the stories we tell that impede us from doing so.

The stories we tell, stories sharing our own experiences and the experiences of others who have had an impact on us, matter a great deal. Having valued others' stories deeply, I feel it seems right to offer a few of my own, in the hope that they may be helpful to you. For if nothing else, I am the internationally recognized leading authority on my own experience. Having lived through what is likely well more than half of my life story, I have wrestled with my own sense of call and capacity for impact, both intellectually and practically, by experimenting with getting in the game in various ways. I imagine that you have too.

In reflecting on my own particular experiences and the public discourse surrounding these topics of activism, impact, and calling, I have come to believe that we could do a better job with this conversation. We often begin the conversation with dubious and unexamined assumptions and then proceed by asking questions that are not particularly enlightening or helpful.

This book challenges some of those assumptions and offers some different questions. Perhaps some of the threads of these stories and ideas will weave into your own story and ideas and free you to have more of a positive impact.

Now a caution about a few things that this book is *not* intended to be.

It is not a strategy book. It is not intended to teach people how to mount effective social justice campaigns. There are some excellent books out there along those lines (I am particularly impressed with Bill Moyer's *Doing Democracy*), but this is not one of them. This is a book about internalized social narratives, and about challenging and changing the stories we typically tell ourselves and each other, some of which keep us paralyzed in the face of problems we could actually address if it weren't for our sense of inadequacy and impotence. Before we have the conversation about *how* we are to go about influencing the world around us, we need to address the bigger question of whether influencing and changing the world is even possible. It seems clear that, whether consciously or subconsciously, many people do not believe that it is. I would like to contest that.

The book is also not a memoir, though I include quite a few stories that arise from my own personal experience. Since mine is the life story I know best, I find that I have often *lived* stories that illustrate the ideas I'm exploring, and I have enjoyed writing them down here.

This is also not a book about politics, at least not in the usual sense. As we are endlessly reminded, we live in a particularly politically divisive time (though I'm not entirely convinced that there has ever been a time that was not politically divisive).

Politics is a blurry word, though. Here in the United States, it has come to mean the contest between the two major political parties. It often appears (and is occasionally blatantly admitted) that their primary goals are not to serve the nation but to defeat the other party. Though I am a strong advocate of political engagement, I am not terribly interested in party loyalty, and I hope that folks of many political perspectives will find value in this book.

In a broader sense, though, the political process—however flawed it may be—is the process by which we make decisions together about *what* matters and *who* matters. That definition includes not only the formal workings of government, but also public discourse, formal and informal media, individual participation through various direct and indirect means, and various forms of influence and power being wielded—appropriately or inappropriately—by the business world, non-profit organizations, civic groups, and others. That kind of politics interests me very much, and it is my duty and yours to be involved in that, no matter what country we live in.

To say that this kind of politics interests me, though, is not the same thing as saying I like it. Like dentistry, the consequences of ignoring it are far worse than the pain of being involved. Where that analogy breaks down, of course, is that, unlike dentistry, if you ignore politics, it is not only you who suffers. As activists and organizers Alexia Salvatierra and Peter Heltzel point out in their book *Faith-Rooted Organizing*, "Democracy doesn't function effectively unless the people participate as active citizens—which is why we call our legislators 'representatives.' As surely as children's behavior reflects on their families, our legislators' behavior reflects on our communities."

That said, this book does not seem to me to be the right forum for arguing my political opinions, in the sense of positions on controversial topics. My political leanings, like my theology, will show through in places, I'm sure; and that doesn't bother me too much, but I hope that no one will be put off by perceived differences in positions. It is not my intention to proselytize about either my faith or my politics, but to share what I have learned about how change really happens and how we can work for a better world together.

I. THE LANGUAGE OF CHANGE

1

Changing My World

Tell me, what is it you plan to do with your one wild and precious life?

—Mary Oliver

I knew I was a real "road dog" not when I first woke up in a hotel and didn't know in which town I was, but when I woke up, didn't know, wasn't concerned about it, and simply went ahead with my shower.

I have spent more than three decades on the road as a touring musician and songwriter, performing in all fifty of the states in the U.S. and on five of the seven continents. Not knowing where I was had stopped surprising me; I knew it would come to me later.

Mornings have never been my specialty. Or rather, I prefer for them to come at the end of my day after a long night of music. Sunrises are a lovely transition to going to bed. The experience of growing comfortable with not knowing where I was when I awoke, though, spoke more to the amount of time I was spending on the road than it did to my usual morning brain fog.

I wasn't in a hotel when I woke up on the morning of January 9, 2001. I was staying with my longtime friend Ann and her family. Though I did feel a bit disoriented, I knew these things: 1) I was in my friend's guest room in Leander, Texas, just north of Austin, well into a concert tour that was taking me across the South and over into New Mexico; 2) It was late morning, and the sun was cutting in through the blinds; and 3) I didn't feel very good.

I had gone to dinner the night before with my friend Kristin, and by the time I woke up, Ann and her daughter Ellen, then a senior in high school, had left for work and school. I wrote in my journal a bit, took a shower, threw some clothes on, and got out my laptop to do a bit of bookkeeping. In those days, people still bought lots of CDs at concerts, so the morning after a concert usually involved some bookkeeping. One not-so-glamorous side of being a professional independent musician is that in the eyes of the IRS, I run a small business, with all of the attendant number crunching. It's not very rock star, but it's a necessary part of the work that I treasure so deeply, so I don't mind the routine.

This particular day, however, was not to be routine.

As I got down to work plugging sales numbers into a spreadsheet, something strange began to happen. When I looked at the computer, I realized I was having a hard time seeing what was on the screen. It was as though I had been staring at a light bulb and had a ghost image obscuring a spot near the middle of my vision. Looking at an individual cell in the spreadsheet seemed too difficult.

From where I had been sitting on the couch, there was a bright window behind the computer screen, making it hard to see. I thought that might be the problem, so I moved; but I still couldn't see the screen very well. I was also beginning to feel nauseous, and I started to wonder if I might have picked up a bug. I felt worse with each passing minute, so I gave up on the computer work.

Thinking it might calm my body and brain a bit, I ran a bath, but that only made me feel more nauseated. And then things got even stranger. My arms began to go numb. It was as though they were asleep, but without the tingling of reawakening. I could use them, clumsily, but I couldn't feel much of anything. That lasted about twenty minutes, then gradually subsided. I started to get nervous. The flu had never done *that* to me before.

Ann was at work, and I didn't have her number there, so I called Kristin to ask for it. I told her what was going on, and she gave me the number. Because I was feeling disoriented, I wanted to make sure that I had written the number down right. I read it back to her, but I read it out wrong, and she corrected me.

I tried again. To this day, I still believe I had written the digits down correctly; but somehow when I went to read them back to her, I was saying them incorrectly. It was as though I couldn't remember what the individual numbers were called. The numbers' names were jumbled. Kristin got scared, and so did I. She called Ann, and Ann called me.

While Ann was racing home from the city, my arms went numb again. As before, it lasted about twenty minutes. Before Ann got home, her daughter Ellen arrived home from high school. Ellen, who is now a physician, told me later that I was trying to talk to her but making no sense—I pointed to a chair and said 'wedding.'

Ann is a strong woman, doing her part to uphold the proud lineage of butt-kicking Texas matriarchs from whom she is descended. She's a good person to have around in a crisis. We had become friends through the Kerrville Folk Festival, a magical mecca for songwriters and acoustic music enthusiasts that runs for eighteen days each year on a big, dusty ranch in the gentle Hill Country west of San Antonio. We had camped there together each year for over a decade and kept in touch through the rest of the year. Over time, she had become like a sister to me, and as her two daughters grew up, they had become good friends as well. I had the honor of officiating at Ellen's wedding a few years ago.

On the day in question, though, I wondered if these relationships and every other personal connection in my life might be rushing to a close. Ann got me in the car and blazed down the highway, talking on the phone with the emergency room at the nearest hospital.

On the way there, I tried to figure out what was happening to me. I was gradually losing my ability to use language, I was throwing up, and my arms kept going numb. Stroke? Brain tumor? Aneurysm? Multiple Sclerosis? I couldn't come up with any hypothesis that wasn't catastrophic, and things were rapidly getting worse.

When I asked Ann to tell me her name, she got really scared. I had been trying to think of it and couldn't, which was ridiculous. She was not just a casual friend. I didn't want to scare her, but it was both frustrating and terrifying that I couldn't get to it, so I asked her, and I managed to make the question understood.

She said, "David, it's Ann. I'm your good friend, and I'm taking you to the hospital."

I already understood everything but her name, though; and at that point, I realized that I wasn't having too much trouble thinking, per se, it was just that the labels were all mixed up. I knew where I was and who I was with, but words weren't working for me. It wasn't as though I were drunk or losing consciousness; the primary neurological symptom was simply that I was losing access to language. I would later learn that this is called *aphasia*.

It seemed unlikely to me that this accelerating dysfunction was going to slow down or reverse. Therefore, it was likely that this was effectively the end of my life as I had known it. I might be accelerating toward a vegetative state of losing mental capacity and use of my limbs, or I might simply be dying, but in that moment, it seemed impossible that things would ever return to what I had known as normal.

Ann squealed into the driveway of the emergency room, where we were met by a bearded nurse with a wheelchair who immediately started asking me questions as he moved me bodily into the chair.

I could still speak, though incoherently, but I couldn't answer, "What's seven plus three?" or tell him where my parents live.

Meanwhile, Ann was talking a blue Texan streak, laying down the law with the nurse, insisting that drugs were not a part of this, and that they shouldn't waste time eliminating that possibility.

The next few hours were hazy for me. I was quite dehydrated, and they put two bags of saline solution in my arm. They performed CAT scans, blood work, and a spinal tap, checking for each of the possible conditions I had thought of and a couple more that would be equally dire. Gradually, I lost the ability to speak altogether, stopped throwing up, and lost consciousness.

After a few hours, I woke up again, and while I was still disoriented and having language issues, things seemed to be less severe. As it turned out, the shape of this day was not a simple slope into complete dysfunction but a bell curve, and the symptoms I had experienced gradually subsided over the next few hours.

Aside from a sore back and headache from the spinal tap, I was mostly fine by the next morning. The doctor said that what I had experienced was a "complex migraine." Migraines, I learned, are not necessarily headaches at all. Headaches are just a common symptom. A migraine is a neurological condition which, according to the doctor who treated me that day, arises from spasms in the brain's blood vessels which prevent blood from getting to some parts of the brain. Other doctors argue that it is more of an electrical storm. A complex migraine, my doctor explained, is a migraine that results in neurological dysfunction.

What happened to me that day was certainly among the more dramatic events of my life. It was terrifying and bizarre, and then it was over. The next day I drove out of town in Dan the Tan Van, my beloved Chevy Astro, heading for New Mexico, where I had another couple of concerts booked.

One of the things I love about life on the road is the balance between that intensely interactive, vulnerable time with people at concerts and the complete solitude of driving for hours the next day. These days, driving that much raises important questions of one's carbon footprint; but if it weren't for that, I would drive long distances for the sheer joy of it. Sometimes I long for the bygone tradition of Sunday afternoon family drives, hitting the road purely for the intrinsic value of the trip. As an introvert in an extroverted line of work, I need that road time to process, muse, and ponder so that I'm ready to be fully present with the people I encounter in the next town and so that I can try to figure out what the day's conversations and experiences meant for me, my art, and my spirit.

Driving down the long, straight highways of West Texas and New Mexico after that terrifying day in Austin, I had time to consider what

Dan the Tan Van, my road companion in those days

had happened and its significance. I spent nearly two weeks musing about my medical misadventure before I wrote about it (I was a "proto-blogger," beginning to write periodic Notes from the Road on my Web site—ironically, about three weeks before a man named John Barger coined the word *weblog* in December 1997).

The migraine experience had changed me in several ways. First, I had spent a few hours thinking that my life was coming to a close, and I'd had time to consider what that meant to me. What struck me as I reflected on that experience was that, though I was certainly scared, I felt no sense of injustice, even in the dramatic moments when I thought I might be dying; I wasn't disappointed with the life I had lived up until then. While I wasn't eager to die at the age of thirty-two, I couldn't complain that I hadn't had a rich ride. I was basically content. Even now, more than twenty years later, that's a good thing for me to remember. I celebrate the intervening years as "bonus time." It's as if I got an extra life in a video game, except it's a real life.

> The two things that had been taken from me that day were my *hands* and my *words*.

The second and more unusual insight that grew out of that day's experience was much deeper for me. When I was gradually losing control and contact, I had a perception of my mind receding from me. It was such a vivid image that it almost appeared to be happening in physical space. As I was losing consciousness in the hospital, there was something that seemed to be moving away from me in the darkness, like a ball of flickering blue light, which I understood to be my own intellect—my capacity for thought and reason.

What is interesting about that is that *my* perspective was not from within that mind looking back; my *mind* was moving away from *me*. What was left was not logic and thought but existence. It was my deepest identity. My best interpretation is that this was my spirit, the deepest place that defines me. And for the first time in my life, I could almost tangibly perceive that as separate and distinct from my thinking mind. There was and is a deep comfort for me in having that almost visceral experience of my own spiritual identity—not what I think, but who I am when words, logic, and calculation have been stripped away.

The third observation, though, is the one that brings me to write this book. I couldn't help but notice that the two things that had been taken from me that day were my *hands* and my *words*.

At the time, I was celebrating my first decade of making a living by playing guitar and singing self-penned songs. It was powerful for me to consider that on that day, it was these two things in particular that I had lost: my ability to hold a guitar and feel the tips of my fingers pressing into steel strings and my capacity to choose and use words, whether for their meaning or their musicality. The extremely personal tools of my art and my trade had been taken away.

And then they were returned.

The question may as well have been written in neon in the sky: "What will you do with these hands and these words?" Or, as the poet Mary Oliver famously wrote, "Tell me, what is it you plan to do with your one wild and precious life?" I had been wrestling with that question in a more general and ambiguous sense for many years, but now it was suddenly brought into searing clarity, forcing me to interrogate my own days and the motivations that drove how I filled them. It was another gift to me, if a painful one; and I continue to receive it and feel its sting.

I suspect that very few of us find that our beliefs and our actions match up neatly. I certainly had seen a gulf between the two in my own life, and this experience forced me to face it head on. In the years since that misadventure in Texas, I've reoriented my life somewhat, wrestling with my own sense of call and exploring where my own joy and gifts can be useful in the world.

For a decade—my entire adult life at that point—I had been traveling around singing hopeful songs about better ways to live our lives, be present, and love each other—and I think that matters. Music can open our hearts in ways that words by themselves seldom can. But I wanted to explore more direct forms of change.

Gradually, I became more active in seeking out ways to have a more tangible positive impact on the world around me, and one small step led to others. In 2004, my wife, Deanna, and I co-founded a non-profit that supports school and library projects in Guatemala. In 2008, I suspended my music career and moved to Australia to pursue a master's degree in International Studies, Peace, and Conflict Resolution as a Rotary World Peace Fellow. The following year, I spent three months in rural southern India, working with a Gandhian sustainable development organization. In 2011, I began a six-year stint on the American Friends Service Committee (AFSC)'s Nobel Peace Prize Nominating Committee. I worked with the North Carolina Council of Churches as their program associate for peace. In recent years, I have been doing a lot more speaking and writing in an effort to encourage people to address the problems they see rather than just complain about them. More recently, I've gone to jail a couple of times for nonviolent civil disobedience, protesting misguided policies that are hurting people in the state where I live, North Carolina. In the midst of all this, I've engaged in many smaller and less dramatic efforts, as most of us do.

My medical mishap, though terrifying, was a gift to me. It made me seriously evaluate my life. A sudden, striking awareness of the finitude of one's life naturally leads to questions about how one should spend it. And of course, the question of what one *should* do leads directly to the question of what one *can* do.

Like most people, I suspect, I open the paper or click through the news online with a sense of malaise that sometimes borders on despair. The problems we face—as individuals, as families, as communities, as nations, and as a planet—are significant, large, and insidious. It is sometimes hard to imagine how *anyone* can have much of an impact, much less how *I* can.

Beyond this sense of overwhelming paralysis, even if we can imagine engaging, questions remain regarding how and where to begin. Where should I start? What's most important? In a world full of need, what, specifically, should *I* do? We will wrestle with those questions and others in the following pages, but I don't pretend that they are easy questions to answer.

I do believe, however, that you can have a significant impact. Not the general "you," but the specific one. That's not a starry-eyed, hopeful-but-naive statement; it is a conclusion I have been led to through years of wrestling with the questions that inspired this book. I know it to be true for many reasons, some of which are laid out in the chapters that follow. Our cultural assumptions about our individual roles in steering large-scale change, how change comes about, and who causes that change are often misguided. I want to spend some time turning these assumptions over and holding them up to the light to see whether they are true or not—and, with that knowledge, how they should influence our daily choices.

Though this book endeavors to be an honest, reality-based look at how things change and what we can hope to accomplish, it is also unapologetically hopeful. Part of my goal is to suggest that those two characteristics, being honest and hopeful, are not necessarily mutually exclusive.

Historian Howard Zinn argues in the first chapter of his *People's History of the United States* that objectivism should not be a goal for historians. All historians necessarily bring their own "selection, simplification, [and] emphasis" to their subject matter, he suggests. He goes on to suggest that the most honest approach to presenting history is to clearly state one's own biases and goals. Starting from the same set of facts, each of us naturally tends to see different pieces as important and emphasize those.

> Our most dangerous threat, in the end, is apathy.

With that in mind, I will explicitly name my own agenda: I want my son and the rest of his generation to grow up in a world that is growing and healing rather than one that is tearing itself apart socially, politically, and physically.

In order to accomplish that, I need to convince you to lend your energy to creating that world. The best way I know to do that is to write this book. In it, I hope to 1) challenge some wrongheaded ideas about how change happens, 2) convince you of your own capacity to have an impact, and 3) offer some questions to help you discern your own callings—how and where you can offer your gifts and energy to a movement of people trying to shift things in healthier and more sustainable directions.

I am not, however, trying to win you over to my causes or positions. This book doesn't seek to recruit you to any causes but your own (assuming those causes are generally intended to make the world around you a better place), though I do unabashedly hope to recruit you to those. I don't know what you are passionate about, but I believe that if more of us actually take action on the issues that concern us, we will all be better off. Our most dangerous threat, in the end, is apathy.

2

What Are You Talking About?

We believe that we know something about the things themselves when we speak of trees, colors, snow, and flowers; and yet we possess nothing but metaphors for things—metaphors which correspond in no way to the original entities.

—Friedrich Nietzsche

Communication is a miracle. Even to speak to a friend in the same room, patterns of sound—variations in amplitude and frequency, thick and thin waves of air, produced by complex biological processes involving tiny patterned electrical pulses and chemical signals triggering subtle muscle contractions and expansions—travel from mouth to ear, where they are decoded and structured into words. These words, in turn, are fairly arbitrary code systems for meanings (of which most words have several), which are strung together to represent ideas.

It is not surprising that we sometimes misunderstand each other; it is shocking that we ever communicate effectively at all.

The German philosopher Johann Georg Hamann took it even farther, saying, "Language is not only the foundation for the whole faculty of thinking, but the central point also from which proceed the misunderstandings of reason by herself." In other words, even in our own minds, even without external communication, words not only give us the tools to think, they are also the main thing that trips us up.

Because of that, I think it may be worthwhile to define a few of the central terms in this book, not because they are complex and arcane, but because they are so common that we seldom take the time to consider exactly what we mean when we use them. Each of the words I want to consider has multiple meanings in English, and my point in taking a quick look at them is not to argue that one definition is the correct one but simply to outline what *I* mean when I use them in this context, in the hope of diminishing the chances that you will misunderstand me.

Hope & Optimism

Václav Havel was the last president of Czechoslovakia and the first president of the Czech Republic. He was a successful poet and playwright as well as a dissident activist— the leader of the country's nonviolent transition from Communism to democracy that came to be known as the "Velvet Revolution." It is rare for a true artist and poet also to be a head of state, and Havel offered a great deal of wisdom from that extremely unusual vantage point.

Against this fraught political background, he said: *"Hope is not prognostication, it is an orientation of the spirit."* Hope, in Havel's estimation, has nothing to do with prediction. "Hope is definitely not the same thing as optimism," he wrote. "It is not the conviction that something will turn out well, but the certainty that something makes sense, regardless of how it turns out."

Hope is the conscious decision to live toward the world you would like to see, to take action to move closer to a better way, regardless of your chances of achieving your goal. The historian Howard Zinn writes:

> To be hopeful in bad times is not being foolishly romantic. It is based on the fact that human history is a history not only of competition and cruelty but also of compassion, sacrifice, courage, kindness... The future is an infinite succession of presents, and to live now as we think human beings should live, in defiance of all that is bad around us, is itself a marvelous victory.

Living in hope is not a matter of believing that things will be OK, or even that the good guys eventually win. Hope begins with an honest assessment of a given situation, but it grows into a conscious choice to lend your own energy to move that situation in a better direction. It is an "orientation of the spirit," and the movements of our spirits inevitably inform our tangible actions. *Orientation* implies direction, which way you intend to move.

Hope, it seems to me, is both an active choice and a choice to be active.

Activist & Protestor

What do you picture when you hear the word *activist*? I have asked this question to audiences in hundreds of workshops and found that the first six or eight images people name consistently include marching, holding signs, and shouting. What affect, what emotional tone, comes to mind when you hear the word *activist*? For many of the people I ask, the first thing they say is *angry*.

So there it is: an activist is an angry protestor, marching in the street holding a sign. That is our commonly held understanding of the word.

There is no question that marching is one example of activism, and that there is a time and place to make signs and head for the streets. I have certainly done that and will very likely do it again. There is also a time for

> Hope, it seems to me, is both an active choice and a choice to be active.

anger and for righteous indignation. But I want to be abundantly clear that when I say *activist*, this is not what I mean.

An *-ism*, according to Merriam-Webster, is "the act, practice, or process of doing something." Their first definition for *active* is "doing things that require physical movement and energy."

So activism is, more or less, the act of doing something that requires physical movement and energy. In other words, taking some action. Any action. *Active-ism* is the opposite of *passive-ism*, doing nothing in the face of a problem.

In this book, when I say *activism* I mean taking any action whatsoever to address a problem that exists outside of yourself (if the problem is internal, it's personal growth). Whether that's talking to the manager at the grocery store about a problem with accessibility, donating to an organization you believe in, visiting the elderly man down the street because he seems to be cut off from his community, getting a group of neighbors together to talk about a problem facing your neighborhood, writing a letter to the editor, or clicking an online petition—if you are taking any action at all to address a problem external to yourself, you are already an active-ist. You are choosing to take action rather than being passive.[1]

The stereotypical image of an angry activist marching in the street or chained to a gate or tree is so pervasive that it can be hard to replace in our own minds. This is not, however, the only, or even the most common, way to be active.

The word *protest* is often equated with *activism*, but protest is actually only one half of activism. Standing in the way of what you think is wrong is sometimes extremely important, but if we do not create and model a better way, the vacuum created by the absence of an oppressive system can lead to an even more oppressive one. Offering an alternative can have even greater impact than interrupting a toxic one.

Since 1976, Habitat for Humanity has been demonstrating an alternative model for creating accessibility to homeownership for people with moderate incomes. Their policy of not accepting interest on the loans they offer to homeowners and instead requiring "sweat equity"—working on their own homes and others'—provides a stark contrast to conventional financial systems. It is important to challenge predatory lending, but it may be even more significant to create compassionate alternative systems.

Abraham Jam, a musical trio of which I'm a part, is trying to do something similar by modeling a partnership between a Muslim, a Jew, and a Christian, literally and figuratively singing in harmony. That harmony also provides a picture that contrasts with the images we generally see regarding relationships between those faith groups.

---

[1]*Passive-ism* should not be confused with *pacifism,* though it often is. Pacifism comes from the Latin *pax,* meaning peace, and *facere,* meaning "to do or to make," so pacifism literally means "making peace," or "doing peace." *Facere* is the fundamental action verb of Latin, like *hacer* in Spanish or *faire* in French. Therefore, pacifism is fundamentally active; it is impossible to be a passive pacifist. Passive, by contrast, comes from the Latin *pati,* meaning "to suffer", which is what people tend to do when they are passive in the face of serious problems.

Both Habitat for Humanity and Abraham Jam are examples of what the political theorist Carl Boggs called *prefigurative movements*, in that they seek to embody the principles for which they are arguing, rather than just demanding external change. The Occupy Movement and Black Lives Matter provide other examples. Their intentional choices to organize in non-hierarchical ways set them apart from many movements for social change, and provided both examples and experiments for how that can be done. Fiercely embodying the values that we are fighting for is a fundamentally different approach to social change from simply attacking that which we oppose, using the same methods that our opposition uses.

In his fascinating book, *The Quiet Before: On the Unexpected Origins of Radical Ideas*, Gal Beckerman writes in detail about the danger of oppositional activism in the absence of prefigurative activism. One of the most compelling case studies he presents is the Egyptian Arab Spring, in which social media protests led to in-person protests that brought down the Egyptian government in February, 2011.

Sadly, the broad coalition that gathered in Tahrir Square was either not willing or not able to create an alternative government in the aftermath of the Mubarak regime. As Beckerman writes, "They were allergic to the practicalities of doing politics."

"When the moment clearly called for protest," Beckerman writes, "they knew what to do. They could zero in on a point of outrage and motivate people to gather around it... [but the] revolutionaries never got quite organized enough."

Beckerman quotes Mahmoud Salem, one of the Tahrir revolutionaries who did try to enter politics, writing about the aftermath of the protests: "Running for office meant you were a power-hungry sell-out... It was an incessant rejectionism. No one seemed interested in building." Meanwhile, the Muslim Brotherhood moved methodically to establish power and structure and ended up with both, returning the country to many of the toxic patterns that the revolutionaries were contesting.

While dramatic and oppositional actions are sometimes essential, they are ineffective without offering an alternative plan. If you are called to the work of building something better, that doesn't mean you are not an activist. Activism takes many forms.

I suspect that if you've read this far, you are the kind of person who has taken at least some action in your life to address a problem. So please understand that when I use the word *activist,* I am referring to *you.*

Anger & Hatred

Many people do not distinguish between anger and hatred or consider them points on a continuum, with hatred being an extreme form of anger. That is not what I mean when I use these words.

Anger is an emotion. It often arises in response to a perceived injustice, and that is a natural and understandable response—maybe even laudable. Our anger may be directed at an unjust situation, at a person or institution that is maintaining or encouraging an injustice, or even at ourselves for our passivity in the face of injustice. In and of itself, anger is natural, and it is not a bad thing. For the most part, we don't choose how we feel, and we are not responsible for those feelings. We are entirely responsible, however, for what we do with them. Anger can be a powerful motivator for constructive action, at least for a little while. Over time, it tends to calcify into hatred.

> Anger is an important place to visit from time to time, but a pretty rotten place to live.

In other words, anger is an important place to visit from time to time, but a pretty rotten place to live.

Hatred, as opposed to anger, involves wishing harm. It is entirely possible to be very angry with someone you love, but to hate someone is in direct contrast with loving them. Love and hatred cannot coexist. Passionate infatuation and hatred, yes. But love and hatred are mutually exclusive. Love and anger, on the other hand, are actually quite a powerful combination when it comes to moving the world around you in a better direction.

Love & Affection

That brings us to one of the most ambiguous and broadly defined words I know: *love.* I use this word to describe how I feel about my parents, how I feel about my wife, and how I feel about Indian food. Civil rights heroes in the United States also used the word *love* to describe their disciplined response to police and others who beat and abused them as they engaged in nonviolent civil disobedience. These are drastically different definitions.

In casual conversation, we tend to use the word *love* to describe a point on a continuum of affection. At one end there is loathing; a bit over from that is dislike; indifference is in the middle; then like, and at the far end, love.

This is *not* the kind of love I'm talking about when I use the word in this book. The way I use it here, love is not an emotion at all.

As with *hope*, when I use the word *love* in this book, I am referring to a choice rather than a feeling. Love is the active and ongoing decision to hold up another's well-being and dignity, regardless of how you feel about that person. It is about how we treat people, sometimes not *because* of our feelings but rather *in spite* of them.

I don't want to deny that it is entirely possible to nourish and cultivate certain emotions. Leaders of nonviolent resistance efforts in the U.S. civil rights movement trained vigorously so that they could learn to redirect their feelings and to perceive the humanity in people, even in those actively doing them harm, and, yes, to *feel* love for their oppressors.

> The way I use it here, love is not an emotion at all.

John Lewis was a student leader in the U.S. civil rights movement and one of the primary organizers of the Nashville lunch counter sit-ins in 1960. After meeting Fellowship of Reconciliation organizer Jim Lawson, who taught them about nonviolence, Lewis and his compatriots trained vigorously for a full year before they acted out their famous transforming initiatives, sitting at "Whites only" lunch counters and refusing to leave when asked. Years later, Lewis used this same training to continue to march forward nonviolently even as state police were beating him and others with batons on the Edmund Pettus bridge in Selma. The ability to feel love for one's opponents and even attackers was fundamental to his understanding and practice of nonviolence. In his 2012 book *Across That Bridge*, Lewis described training for civil disobedience:

> For those of us who accepted [nonviolence] not simply as a tactic but as a way of authentically living our lives—our sole

purpose was, in fact, love. We would settle for the proceeds of justice and equal rights, but the force guiding our involvement was the desire to redeem the souls of our brothers and sisters who were beguiled by the illusion of superiority, taken in and so distorted by their false god that they were willing to destroy any contradiction of that faith. If we were pawns of an unjust system, they were also so complicit in their own degradation that they justified wrong as a service to the right.

Lewis and others got to that place by cultivating their compassion (which etymologically means "suffering with") in order to perceive the humanity of their oppressors. Through rigorous training and study, he and his colleagues in the struggle learned to *feel* differently about people who were doing them harm. That's extraordinary, especially when you remember that these words were spoken by a man who was beaten bloody and unconscious on many occasions, not only on that infamous day in Selma.

But that's a high bar to set, and quite a dramatic context in which to examine nonviolence. That kind of moral ascendance and physical sacrifice is not what I'm asking of you or myself in this book, at least not as a starting place. So many of these heroic stories in the history books leave out the years of small, incremental steps and practice that led ordinary people to such heroic actions, and overemphasize the dramatic at the expense of the practical. I don't want to make the same mistake here.

As a starting place, I think it is enough to ask ourselves to love people through our actions—including speech, gesture, and expression—whether or not we can summon the feelings to go with that.

It may well be that the emotional perspective of love will follow the lived experience. As Father Richard Rohr of the Center for Action and Contemplation is fond of saying, "we do not think ourselves into new ways of living, we live ourselves into new ways of thinking." I suspect that is what happened with Lewis and his companions. For now, though, let's bite off a chewable piece. Acting in love, regardless of how we feel, is hard enough, and it's a sufficient goal. The danger in asking too much of ourselves is that when we are not able to achieve immediately what our heroes achieved over many years, we will be immobilized by a sense of inadequacy.

What is abundantly clear, at any rate, is that loving someone is not simply an extreme version of liking them. In fact, we are sometimes called to love people we don't like at all.

Aid & Justice

The best story I've heard to illustrate the difference between aid work and justice work has been told by many different people with slight variations, and I'm not sure to whom it should be originally attributed. Here's what happens in the story:

One day a woman was taking a walk. Enjoying the solitude and peace of strolling beside a river, she heard a splashing sound and turned her head to see whether a duck was landing or a fish jumping.

Instead, she was shocked to find a human baby floating down the river. It was thrashing and trying to breathe and clearly in great danger. Immediately, she plunged into the cold river and retrieved the baby. She brought it to the bank and tried to warm and comfort it while it choked out water and cried, all the while looking around for some explanation or someone else to help.

Then she heard another splash and turned around to see another baby floating down the river. She was doubly shocked, but the situation demanded quick action, so she set the first baby down on the riverbank and dove back into the water to get the second baby.

She hadn't even made it back to the shore when a third baby came floating downstream. This time, though, someone else was coming along the path, so she shouted out for him to come help while she plunged back into the cold river for the third rescue.

The woman quickly informed the man what was happening, and before she was done explaining what little she knew, sure enough, here came a fourth baby. The man had a phone and started calling friends to come down and bring blankets, towels, formula, and whatever else they could think of. In the meantime, the two of them continued to pull babies from the river.

Over time, lots of people came to help. They brought bassinets and tents and diapers, but the babies kept coming, so eventually they started raising money and built a permanent structure beside the river to deal with the steady flow of babies. Before long, they had developed a solid volunteer crew, reliable donors, and a long-term plan for feeding and housing the babies. They obtained their 501(c)3 tax exempt status, and put together a board of directors. They had almost started to feel as if they were catching up when one day an older woman walked into the building, looked around with a stern expression, threw her head back, and shouted for everyone to stop and be quiet.

> Aid work is about meeting people's needs. Justice work is about challenging the systems that make people needy.

Shocked, they all did so, and when she had everyone's full attention, she looked around the room and firmly but quietly said, "Don't you think it's time we went upstream to see who is throwing them in?"

That story, while fictitious, provides a helpful illustration of the difference between aid work and justice work. Aid work is about meeting people's needs. Justice work is about challenging the systems that make people needy.

I should also say that I have sometimes heard this story told with an implication that justice work is the wiser, nobler, and more effective path. But I question that. If everyone at the baby shelter had stopped what they were doing and marched upstream, the babies already in the river that day would have drowned.

Both are necessary. The former tends to be more short term and the latter more long term, but they both have the potential to serve people who need help and support.

Aid and justice work can also overlap and be mutually supportive. I've found that this is sometimes the case with communities working with people who have no housing. Some of these communities take on both the work of helping people find what they need for material sustenance and safety, and of educating and challenging local governments and the larger society on the problems and their structural causes.

My friends at the Open Door Community in Atlanta, for example, were growing weary of bailing their friends out of jail for urinating in alleys. As Ed Loring at the Open Door tells it, the city had no public toilets until 2000. That meant that people who had no homes and no money to spend in businesses that might allow them access to bathroom facilities also had nowhere to relieve themselves. When they did what was necessary, they were arrested, despite having no other practical options.

The Open Door community not only made their homes available to people needing showers and toilets, they also began to advocate for more public toilets. On several occasions in the nineties, they marched down to the City Hall and had demonstrations, giving speeches, singing, and reading scripture in Mayor Andrew Young's office while seated on a porcelain perch that they had brought with them. They worked to meet people's needs and at the same time challenged the systems that made them needy (and they did so with a sense of humor). Eventually, more people took up the cause, and finally the city built public toilets.

These days it seems to be fashionable to lionize justice work and denigrate aid work. There are certainly plenty of examples of aid work that further marginalizes people who are theoretically being served. Stories of aid organizations that inadvertently categorize everyone involved into "helper" or "helped," or charities that serve from a distance without sharing stories and human fellowship, are not hard to find, and those approaches are problematic.

Poorly realized aid work has the potential to assault dignity and entrench hierarchical systems and values. In my experience, however, poorly executed justice work can damage dignity as well. Both aid and justice work can be carried out in ways that demean all involved and tokenize certain people while celebrating others. Yet both can also foster relationship, nourish dignity, and address problems in meaningful, sustainable ways that build capacity and mutual respect on all sides.

These two different approaches, sometimes mutually supportive and sometimes in tension, are both necessary. Part of our work is to discern our own roles within each and how to do them both well.

Peace & Placidity

I referred earlier to civil rights hero John Lewis, who headed up the Student Nonviolent Coordinating Committee (SNCC), the student wing of the nonviolent movement led by Dr. Martin Luther King, Jr. From 1987 until his death in 2020, Lewis served as a United States Congressman representing Georgia's fifth congressional district.

In early 2009, just before heading to Australia to begin my master's degree, I had the opportunity to meet and spend some time in conversation with him. Representative Lewis was coming to Western North Carolina, where I live, to speak at the Montreat Conference Center. My friend Wade Burns is a longtime friend of Lewis', having worked on integration issues in Atlanta with him, sometimes in intense and dangerous situations.

Wade was heading to the airport to pick up Representative Lewis and asked me if I wanted to ride along. We met Lewis at the airport and, after a brief reunion of old friends and an introduction, we headed for the parking lot. Representative Lewis wouldn't let either of us help with his bag, nor would he sit in the front when we got to the van. Wade smiled at this and said that he wanted the two of us to have some time for conversation anyway, so John Lewis and I sat together in the back seat and talked, with Wade quietly playing the chauffeur and listening.

> Peace is not placidity, and making peace does not mean making nice.

It was an extraordinary gift to me and a generous thing for Wade to give up that time with his good friend so that we could have a conversation I will never forget. Later that evening, we had dinner together with a few other guests at Wade and Susie's home, but for the duration of the van ride, I had John Lewis to myself. I tried not to waste it.

Representative Lewis wanted to know about me and what I was working on, so I briefly told him about my music and my workshops, my new baby boy, and the fact that I would be packing up my family in a couple of weeks to move to Australia to pursue a master's degree in peace work as a Rotary World Peace Fellow. The conversation naturally turned to peace work and then to some common misunderstandings about that pursuit. Among those misconceptions, we talked about the idea that peace is the lack of conflict.

It was, and sometimes still is, a common criticism of John Lewis, Martin Luther King, Jr., Rosa Parks, and their compatriots in the civil rights movement that they were hardly peacemakers; after all, everywhere they went, conflict and violence seemed to erupt! However, that critique betrays a shallow understanding of the word *peace*.

The kind of peace work in which these people were involved had to do with structural violence—violence that is built into systems and damages people in ways that are equally destructive as, but far more subtle than, direct violence. Preserving the status quo in the presence of injustice or unresolved injury, even where overt violence might be tamped down, can hardly be called peaceful.

Johan Galtung, often considered the founder of the field of peace and conflict studies, is generally credited with coining the terms *positive peace* and *negative peace*. Negative peace is merely the absence of overt violence. Positive peace is the presence of attitudes, systems, and institutions that nourish community and encourage the possibility of healthy living. Negative peace can be a useful step on the way to positive peace, but it is insufficient as the end goal.

> The work of peacemaking is not about ending conflict: it is about approaching conflict in ways that are constructive rather than destructive.

Lewis said to me, "Peace is not the absence of conflict; conflict is often necessary on the way to justice." Those words, coming from a man who had willingly and courageously endured significant physical violence in the service of the pursuit of justice, had the full weight of history behind them.

The other thing Representative Lewis said to me that I will never forget made all the hairs on my arms stand up[2]. He said, "Dr. King used to say to me, 'Sometimes you have to turn the world upside down in order to set it right.'"

Peace is not placidity, and making peace does not mean making nice. Sometimes the work of peacemaking involves *revealing* a conflict that

---

[2]I try to pay attention when that happens, as it's one of the things you can't fake. I consider it a signal that something important is happening.

is woven into a situation. Bringing it out into the open so that we can deal with it. That can look like creating tension. That is why people who work for justice are constantly accused of stirring up trouble. But the trouble was there long before they arrived. In order to heal it, we have to give it light and air. In Rep. Lewis' words, we have to make "good trouble."

Truthfully, the noun *peace* is not nearly as interesting to me as the gerund form: *peacemaking*. I'm not interested in a static, unachievable, utopian ideal as much as I am in discerning what my role is in moving myself and the world around me a bit more in a positive direction.

Conflict is an inevitable part of being human, and it is not necessarily a bad thing. The work of peacemaking is not about ending conflict; it is about approaching conflict in ways that are constructive rather than destructive.

Note that key word in that last sentence is *approaching*.

John Lewis in Montreat, NC

3

Good Luck with That

While I am not optimistic, I am hopeful. By this I mean that hope, as opposed to cynicism and despair, is the sole precondition for a new and better life; and hope arouses, as nothing else can arouse, a passion for the possible.

—William Sloan Coffin

January 20, 2009—a couple of weeks after I met John Lewis—was Inauguration Day in the United States. My wife, Deanna, my friend and office manager MJ, my parents, and I gathered to watch Barack Obama take the oath of office. No matter how one feels about the presidency that followed, that moment was undeniably historic, and for me, it was deeply inspiring.

We watched it in an empty house with almost no furniture remaining, crowding around my laptop, my mother holding our ten-week-old son. We celebrated the election of a candidate who, we believed, would turn the country in a better direction from the one in which we had been heading. Then we closed the laptop, put our suitcases in the car, drove to the airport, and moved to Australia.

President Obama and I were both embarking on new chapters that day, though mine, needless to say, was on a much smaller scale. Many good and bad decisions were yet to come for both of us, but in both cases the day was significant—even with nothing yet accomplished—just because of the choice to begin.

A great deal had already changed for me from the same date two years before. In early 2007, I was celebrating sixteen years on the road as a full-time musician. I had developed a base of listeners on three continents who were coming out to shows, buying my CDs, sending lovely notes from time to time, telling their friends about my music, and supporting me, both financially and as an artist. After getting through the initial inevitable years of starving musicianship, I had something that many musicians more talented than I never get to have—a music career.

I was also married to a smart, strong, kind, and beautiful woman who supported my art while still having her own life and enough confidence in our relationship to allow me to be gone a great deal of the time. In spite of the travel, we agree that we had more "quality time" in those years than most couples do because when I came home, we set aside everything else just to be together.

> In short, things were working. And that's when I decided to walk away.

We were close to having paid for our little house in the mountains of Western North Carolina. We had family nearby and friends with whom to laugh and cry. In short, things were working. And that was when I decided to walk away.

I had heard from a friend about the Rotary Peace Fellowship, a generous academic fellowship for a master's degree in Peace and Conflict Resolution. My friend had just completed a master's degree at the University of Bradford in England through that program, funded by the Rotary Foundation, and it sounded like an extraordinary experience.

I was amazed to learn that such a program existed, but I was even more amazed at my own reaction to hearing about it; against all precedent, it tempted me away from the calling I had been pursuing joyfully for my entire adult life. I certainly had plenty of days when I was weary of the road and the hustle, but overall, I was happy in my work. It is not overstatement to say that I was among the very few musicians whose dream had come true.

Still, it felt as if this was the next chapter for me. Not in a practical sense, but in an almost mystical one. It was simply clear. It was as if

I had come to a corner and could suddenly see around it—and there was the road. This was my path all along, but I couldn't see it until I got to the corner.

To be clear, this direction wasn't completely new. During my undergraduate years in the late eighties, I attended James Madison University in Harrisonburg, Virginia. It wasn't until I had been there a while that I found my real passion: alternative conflict resolution work. I was hooked. I ended up doing an independent study and interning at the Community Mediation Center, where I was exposed to some amazing peacemakers doing substantive work in their own community to help heal wounds in families, between neighbors, in the business community, and elsewhere.

I was deeply impressed with these people and with that experience. I watched the work they did each day, learned about mediation and conflict resolution, helped run training sessions, and even engaged in some mediation myself. I was quickly converted, and I was amazed to discover that there are more effective ways to approach conflict than the ones we usually turn to, though we so seldom use them. Mediation is demonstrably better at resolving most kinds of conflicts than litigation, whether we measure the results in satisfaction of the parties to the conflict, durability of the agreements, or by a variety of other measures; and it is methodical, teachable and learnable.[3] In those days (the late eighties), mediation was just moving into the mainstream, and I became a passionate advocate for it.

It was in those same years, however, that I started performing publicly. I had been playing guitar in the solitude of my bedroom for many years, but in college I worked up the courage to play an open mic, and I was amazed and thrilled to find that people didn't boo me off the stage. As I started to perform more around town, I was even more surprised to realize that people were reacting positively to some of the songs I had written myself, not just the standard canon of folk/pop that made up most of my repertoire in those days. I spent a semester abroad in

---

[3]I'm not intending to pick on lawyers here. An attorney once pointed out to me at the National Conference on Restorative Justice that litigation is already alternative conflict resolution, and he was right. It's a significant step in the right direction from violence and deserves credit as such. Mediation and other forms of restorative justice, I believe, take more healthy steps in the right direction.

Paris in the second half of my junior year and ended up traveling for a few weeks after it was over, playing on street corners to have money for food. And I didn't starve.

When I graduated from college, I felt strongly pulled in two different directions, and the two vocations were incompatible. On the one hand, there was mediation, which had become a passion for me, and it felt like a way that I might have a positive influence in the world. On the other, there was music, an even more unlikely way to make a living, one about which I was equally passionate. In the few years I'd been playing in public, I had occasionally seen tears in the eyes of people listening when I played my own songs. It seemed as if my music might actually matter too.

In the light of some significant encouragement (some of which is outlined in stories which appear later in this book), I decided to give myself two years to see whether I could make a living playing music. After graduation, and a summer job running the tech crew for the Montreat conference center, as I had for two previous summers, I got a side job that didn't require much brain power and didn't run the risk of becoming a passion for me: moving chairs, cleaning, and whatever manual labor was needed at Assembly Inn in Montreat. That is the same hotel where my parents met while working their own summer jobs nearly forty years before. Four months later, as the tourist season wound down, there wasn't much work left for me to do there, and I began my life as a full-time musician.

The trajectory of an independent music career usually doesn't have a lot of spikes in it. It is mostly a matter of longevity, connecting and building relationships with a base of people over many years who relate to what you're doing. Those relationships have sustained me both emotionally and financially through the support of faithful fans and friends who continue to invite me into various opportunities to speak and perform—friends who keep coming to the shows, even though they have heard some of those songs many times before.

My music career is a bit of an anomaly, though. My mother told me that she heard a story on NPR years ago in which they interviewed someone who had done a study to discover how many people who set out to have a career in music actually get to have one. That researcher came up with one in five hundred.

I am that one. For years I made my living by playing self-penned songs for mostly small audiences, traveling in progressively wider circles until I had developed small but passionate followings in this country as well as in Australia, New Zealand, and Germany.

But I never lost my passion for peace work. While I was traveling, I would sometimes go to places where significant conflicts were taking place and meet people who were engaged with those issues on a daily basis.

On one such trip, I went to northern Ireland[4] and met with people doing front-line peace work there, some working with war widows and orphans, others with youth, trying to break down the persistent cultural, political, and historical barriers between Protestants and Catholics.

On another trip, I performed for United Nations peacekeeping troops at Eagle Base in Tuzla, Bosnia, then spent a few days in Sarajevo, where I connected with peacemakers doing reconciliation work in that troubled time and place. I learned what I could by watching and listening, and I offered what I could by playing songs and sharing stories.

> I learned what I could by watching and listening, and I offered what I could by playing songs and sharing stories.

All that time, I continued to look for ways to connect more substantially with peace work, which had remained a passion for me. I couldn't see how it was compatible, though. Mediation requires a steady presence and availability. Music, at least the way I was approaching it, requires a great deal of travel and a lifestyle almost devoid of routine.

So I mostly gave my energy to music, putting out ten CDs over eighteen years and performing about two thousand concerts around the world. Each year went better than the last in terms of opportunities and finances. It was a good life. With the help of an amazing deal from a

[4]This is not a typo. I'm following the lead of my good friend Gareth Higgins from Belfast. Gareth is a peacemaker, author, and film critic. He explains in his excellent book Cinematic States that he chooses not to capitalize the 'N' in northern Ireland, "because we still can't agree on what to call my divided home."

friend and a small inheritance from my grandparents, I began buying a little house. When I met my wife, Deanna, I was even able to help her out with her student loans.

There was no practical reason that I should walk away. After years of living very simply and cheaply, I finally had a bit of breathing room. Still, when I heard about the Rotary World Peace Fellowship, I had to pursue it, though it would be profoundly disruptive.

If I got it, I would have to move to another country. Each year, the Rotary Foundation chooses fifty people from all over the world to pursue master's degrees in Peace Studies or a related field at one of five prominent universities around the world and fifty more to do a three-month certification program in Thailand. The Rotary Foundation generously provides tuition, living expenses, funding for independent field study, and even transportation there and back.

At that point, I didn't even know which of the Rotary World Peace Centers I would attend if selected: in Argentina, Japan, England, or Australia (the rules require that Fellows study in countries other than their own, so the two programs in the U.S. at that time were off limits). More than that, I had no reason to be confident that I would be awarded the fellowship at all, given that applicants had to make it through a rigorous global selection process.[5]

Even so, I announced the beginning of a year-long farewell tour that would take me to many of the places I had come to love as a musician, and that would give me a chance to say some important goodbyes. I felt so strongly drawn to this new path that I announced my "retirement" as a musician, despite the very real possibility that I would not be awarded the fellowship. If I didn't get it, I decided, it was because some other avenue of peace work would open to me. What I knew was that I needed to focus on this work for a while, and to do that, I had to lay down my guitar. I love music too much to do just a little of it on the side, so I knew that if I was going to pursue my other vocation in peace work seriously, it would require my full attention.

I had some friends who supported my new direction. Though some were admittedly unsure, they patted me on the back and wished me

---

[5]The locations of the Rotary Peace Centers have changed over the years, but the program continues. For more information on the Rotary Peace Fellowship, visit rotary.org/en/peace-fellowships.

well. There were others who were baffled and some who expressed misgivings. Others, rather than patting me on the back, patted me on the head, at least figuratively. "Peace work" sounds like a rather silly place to put one's energy, and I had put a lot of work into my music career.

The most common response I got was from well-meaning friends and acquaintances who raised an eyebrow, smiled with an expression that was warm if somewhat sardonic, and said, "Peace? Good luck with that."

As a culture, we have some commonly held beliefs about this idea of working to change the world for the better. Foremost among them is that it is naive. According to the popular narrative, such idealistic effort is born of a childish perspective that people are basically good and reasonable, joined with a sheltered ignorance of the hard cruelty of the "real world." Experience and maturity, the logic goes, will cure the idealists of their foolish delusions.

> As a culture, we have some commonly held beliefs about this idea of working to change the world for the better. Foremost among them is that it is naive.

And the fundamentally chaotic and destructive nature of the world itself seems to support that skepticism. "Look at the world!" the skeptics quite reasonably cry. People have been trying to end war and poverty for centuries, and yet the world is riddled with war and crippled by poverty. The lesson they draw is this: *You can't change the world.*

This sounds so self-evident as to be banal. And how ridiculous does it sound to suggest the opposite? Here's an experiment: Next time you run into a friend at the grocery store, and they ask what you're up to these days, look them in the eyes and say without irony, "Oh, y'know, I'm changing the world."

Their response will likely be some combination of chuckling, nervous subject-changing, and possibly an urgent matter in the produce aisle to which to attend. Such a statement sounds foolish, comical, or slightly unbalanced. Your friend is likely to walk away wondering whether you inhaled too much exhaust on your way in from the parking lot.

The skeptics seem to have a point, don't they? Isn't it naive, even mildly delusional, to think you can change the world?

And even if the world *does* change a bit in response to our efforts, the planet is still dripping with violence.[6] Where is the hope in that?

Hope, peacemaking, and efforts to effect change are not rooted in denial of the gritty reality of the world, though. They are rooted in the observation that we can have a positive impact, and that it is irresponsible and self-defeating not to try.

The nihilist position that we can have no effect, that the world is doomed to chaotic violence despite our best efforts, does not hold up to scrutiny. The cynical assumption that hope and experience are necessarily adversaries does not fare well either, though it is a popular narrative.

Sheltered young people have big dreams, the narrative goes, and then they encounter the world. Once they understand the unspeakable oppression, cruelty, violence, timidity, and selfishness of which human beings are capable, they give up on those dreams. A solid dose of reality cures them of such silliness. They grow out of it.

If that were true, however, then Nelson Mandela, as a well-known purveyor of hope, would have had to be sheltered from the cruelty of the world in order to hold such a worldview. After all, according to the twisted but pervasive logic of the cynics, Mandela would have had to be at best naive to hold such a view—at worst, delusional. Perhaps in his twenty-eighth year of prison, reality would have sunk in; but twenty-seven years as a political prisoner of the apartheid[7] government in South Africa were apparently not enough to convince him that people are hopelessly cruel and unjust.

---

[6]Though arguably less violence than at any other period of history. Steven Pinker argues convincingly in The Better Angels of Our Nature that violence has been in steady decline across millenia, centuries, and decades.

[7]With some agitation and urgency, South African faith-based activist Dave Wanless, who was the Director of Communications for the South African Council of Churches under Desmond Tutu, once interrupted a question I was asking him to correct my pronunciation of apartheid. I was pronouncing it like a German word, with the last syllable rhyming with light, but in Afrikaans, he said, the word is properly pronounced apart-hate. Dave was insistent: "That's important because that's what it was built on: apartness and hate.

A few years ago, I stood with my hands on the bars of Nelson Mandela's prison cell on Robben Island. He slept on the smooth concrete floor for most of his time there, and he and the other political prisoners received less food than the non-political criminals housed elsewhere on the island. The guard dogs kept on the island literally had more space in their private kennels than Mandela had in his cell.

On that same trip, I went to lunch with Father Michael Lapsley, an Anglican priest who had become the chaplain to the ANC, Mandela's political party, during the anti-apartheid movement. Ethan Vesely-Flad, of Fellowship of Reconciliation, had introduced us, and Father Lapsley took time from his work at the Institute for the Healing of Memories[8] to have a conversation with my friend Dr. Vernon Rose and me. We met at his office, chatted there for a few minutes, and then walked a couple of blocks to a local diner.

Father Lapsley is a friendly and sharp-witted man. He smiles easily and doesn't hesitate to poke at pretense, playfully challenging my descriptions of what I'm doing here in South Africa. After I tell him what I'm working on and why, he generously answers a few of my questions.

"There is a perspective that working for change is adolescent," he said. "Some of my colleagues ask, 'Are you still doing that?' as though I should have grown out of it by now. Apparently, we should be drinking scotch and analyzing issues, but not doing anything about them."

---

[8]www.healing-memories.org

with Father Lapsley and Dr. Rose in Cape Town

But there he is, doing the work. And smiling sincerely and amiably as he does so. I don't pretend to know him well, but based on our brief time together, he strikes me as a man at peace and a man of hope. He knows something, after all, about healing.

Father Lapsley moved to South Africa from his native New Zealand in 1973, taking on the chaplaincy of both the White and Black universities in Durban shortly after he arrived. First, he began speaking out on behalf of students who were being shot, arrested, and tortured. Later, he joined the African National Congress and became a chaplain to that organization.

In 1990, three months after Nelson Mandela was released from prison, the security forces of the South African government sent Father Lapsley a letter bomb. That bomb blew off both of his hands and severely damaged one of his eyes.

> Hope is not necessarily maintained by refusing to acknowledge the existence of cruelty and organized oppression. Deep hope is the antithesis of naiveté.

Now he is working with trauma victims worldwide, focusing on victims of the apartheid regime and with United States military veterans through an organization that he founded, the Institute for the Healing of Memories.

Has he held on to his hope because he doesn't understand the capacity of humans to be cruel and heartless? Was losing his hands to his own government's act of terrorism not sufficient to make him see reality?

Was Gandhi hopeful because he didn't understand what he was up against, having watched people he loved march unarmed and hands down into the batons of British troops, who struck them down repeatedly? Or what about Dr. King? Being beaten repeatedly, jailed time after time, having his house firebombed—that was not enough education for him to understand the human capacity for cruelty and evil?

Or could it be that these people had a broader perspective and a deeper understanding? That they understood all along the moral depravity and cruelty that humans can display, and their hope was not predicated on denying it? Could it be that those bright lights had an understanding that reaches beyond our own naiveté? That their worldview is grounded in a reality that encompasses the human capacity for unspeakable cruelty, selfishness, hatred, and violence, but responds with a kinetic hope that—rather than denying that darkness—nourishes the other, equally demonstrable reality of the human capacity for healing, reconciliation, generosity, and empathy?

We don't need to suffer the dramatic sacrifices that these people have suffered to begin to understand what they have tried to teach us. If we have the wisdom to listen to them, we will learn that hope is not necessarily maintained by refusing to acknowledge the existence of cruelty and organized oppression. Deep hope is the antithesis of naiveté.

And yet people of hope, the ones who talk about changing the world and try to do so, are regularly dismissed as being out of touch with reality.

> It is not naive to think you can change the world. In fact, it is naive to think that you can be in the world and not change it.

Imagine being in an anti-apartheid organizing meeting at a U.S. university in the late eighties, when Nelson Mandela was still in jail, the United States government still supported the apartheid regime, and things looked quite bleak in South Africa.

What if you had stood up and said, "OK, here's what's going to happen: Nelson Mandela will be released from prison, and then about four years later South Africa will have free and fair elections in which he will be elected president. There will not be retributive genocide of Whites, and though there will still be many serious issues to deal with, South Africa will largely recover economically and politically. It will end up adopting one of the most progressive constitutions in the world, enshrining civil rights as few have done. I think that's what's going to happen."

How would people in that meeting have responded? I imagine they would have laughed you out of the room as a lunatic or a starry-eyed dreamer.

But who in the room would have been most in touch with reality? Who had the best handle on what would happen in the real world?

As a culture, we seem to have come to a place where we equate cynicism with realism and hope with naiveté. But that is, well, unrealistic. Reality sometimes *is* hopeful, and we need not defeat ourselves before we start. There is, of course, such a thing as naive optimism, but living in hope is something altogether different.

Neither is it naive to think that we can change the world. "Change," remember, is not equivalent to "fix."

If we are talking about *fixing* the world—eliminating all conflict, strife, and injustice—then some eye rolling is unquestionably in order. But it is not naive to think you can *change* the world. In fact, it is naive to think that you can be in the world and *not* change it. Everything you do changes the world whether you like it or not. So the questions we must ask ourselves are, "Which changes will we make?" and, "How will we go about making them?"

II. NARRATIVES OF CHANGE

4

Out of the Blue

The work of the world is common as mud.

—Marge Piercy

Somewhere around 1997, I wandered down to my local music hall, the Grey Eagle. Two guys I knew, Matthew Kahler and Shawn Mullins, had driven up from Atlanta for a concert. They are both great writers and performers, and I didn't want to miss the show.

Neither did the other eleven people who showed up. The Grey Eagle can hold over two hundred people, so twelve was a bit awkward. The sound system and stage lighting seemed sort of silly with such a minimal crowd.

Shawn and Matthew were already seasoned performers in those days, though; they had enough years on the road and enough perspective to appreciate those folks who did come out rather than complain about those who didn't. They did a wise and appropriate thing, and I learned by watching them. They brought their guitars and Matthew's drum down off the stage. They invited the rest of us to make a circle of chairs and sat in the circle with us. Then they played their show, chatting and laughing casually with people between songs and answering questions as they went. I think they may have passed me a guitar and asked me to play a song or two as well. In short, they celebrated and nourished the beautiful intimacy of a small gathering, rather than awkwardly pretending it was a large one.

The next time Shawn came to town, as I recall, he came alone in his pickup truck. Or rather, he came with his little dog, Roadie, in the passenger seat, which was how he usually rolled in those days. The crowd may have been a little bit better, but, as is often the case, it was grossly out of proportion to his talent. Shawn is quite a songwriter and deserved a packed house, as the world would soon discover.

I was packing the Grey Eagle in those days, not in proportion to talent, but because it's my own small town, and folks support me here. Shawn consistently sold out Eddie's Attic in Decatur, his hometown venue; and my crowds there were hardly packed. So Shawn suggested (or maybe I did?) that we trade opening slots for each other at our hometown concert venues so that each of us could be exposed to the other's audience.

A few months later, he came back to town and opened for me in front of a solid crowd. He was great, as he consistently is; people loved his set and bought lots of CDs.

In fact, a lot of people were starting to discover Shawn's music, including a major radio station in Atlanta where, a few months after opening for me, Shawn was charting with his song "Lullaby." Subsequently, some major record labels took interest in the song. The verses are spoken in Shawn's gravelly, accessible poetry, and the choruses soar with his pure falsetto in a juxtaposition that is hard to resist—not just because it's catchy, but because the whole spectrum of sound and emotion in the song is undeniably authentic.

Not too long after being picked up in Atlanta, the song was at #1 on *Billboard*'s Adult Top 40 charts. It spent eight weeks there and charted well in the U.K., Canada, and Australia as well. I thoroughly enjoyed watching that success emerge. Shawn had worked hard at his craft for years, and it was a joy to see that paying off.

I never did get in touch to say so, knowing that for a while, at least, Shawn would have a whole lot of people trying to get a bit closer. I didn't want to be one of the many people who suddenly wanted to claim him as a best friend. Besides, I didn't want him to feel obligated to thank me, since naturally I chalked up most of his success to opening for me in Black Mountain. That had to be the tipping point, right?

Sure enough, life quickly became very busy for Shawn, and, by his own description when we talked about it later, also somewhat surreal. He was flying to New York to appear on talk shows and play concert venues like Madison Square Garden instead of opening for me in Black Mountain.

One night Shawn found himself sitting in the interview chair with Jay Leno on the Tonight Show. Jay opened the interview by saying something along the lines of, "Wow, you came out of nowhere!"

Shawn smiled good-naturedly and said, "Yeah, I guess after ten years on the road, I'm an overnight success." As Shawn recounted it to me, Mr. Leno was surprised by his response, and Shawn had the opportunity to challenge in a gentle way the "overnight success" narrative that we love so much as a nation.

By the time "Lullaby" hit the pop charts, Shawn had been on the road for years. He had studied music formally, led a military band while he was in the service, performed hundreds of concerts, and put out eight independent CDs. That's not overnight.

> We prefer the idea that talented artists are "discovered" and plucked out of obscurity to become stars, somehow skipping over the steady, long-term work of building something valuable.

Shawn's story, however, doesn't fit the narrative we love. As a culture, we prefer the idea that talented artists are "discovered" and plucked out of obscurity to become stars, somehow skipping over the steady, long-term work of building something valuable. It rarely happens that way, but this idea holds so much more appeal than the truth because it means *we* might wake up tomorrow being celebrated by the nation.

We love to apply that narrative to our social justice heroes, too, but it's not true of them either.

Civil rights hero and U.S. Congressman John Lewis did not start out being beaten into a coma on the Edmund Pettus bridge. He started out going to a meeting. A representative of the Fellowship of Reconciliation (FOR) was in town to hold a workshop at a church near Lewis' college, and he went to check it out. The FOR had recently published a comic book about Dr. King and the emerging civil rights movement called *Martin Luther King and the Montgomery Story*,[9] and Lewis was among many students across the South who had read it. He showed up at the meeting with seven or eight other students and listened to a man named James Lawson lead a discussion about nonviolent resistance. Lewis and his fellow students were hooked.

They began meeting every Tuesday night to study justice issues and nonviolence from the fall of 1958 into the fall of 1959. As time went on, they practiced role plays of nonviolent resistance, abusing each other physically and verbally so that they could feel the full weight of what they were up against and prepare themselves to respond nonviolently. Finally, after a full year of study and preparation, they formed the Nashville Student Movement, which orchestrated the sit-ins that desegregated Nashville's lunch counters, then movie theaters, then restaurants.

1957 FOR comic book

Most people in the United States became aware of that movement only when the sit-ins and the subsequent violent responses to them suddenly dominated the nightly news. But it all started with a meeting. Or maybe it started when John Lewis heard Rev. King preaching on the radio, or when he read that comic book. At any rate, it started small.

And for so many people, it *stays* small and undramatic. Please don't misunderstand me: these are not the control group for whom the formula didn't work. They are the ones who drive the movement and bring about the change. Going to a meeting is not necessarily a "gateway" action. It may lead to... well, going to more meetings, writing some letters, and talking with some people. And those undramatic

---

[9]This classic publication has been republished by FOR, and translated into many languages. In addition to its significant influence on the US civil rights movement, it has been influential in modern nonviolent movements as well. For more information, visit forusa.org

actions may matter a great deal in bringing about the changes you seek, not just by setting up the dramatic moments, but by methodically interrupting toxic systems and gradually actualizing new and better ways forward.

The dozen of us who were at Shawn and Matthew's show at the Grey Eagle won't forget it. It moved us and changed us, and it taught me how to approach and honor a smaller-than-hoped-for audience. It wasn't Madison Square Garden, but it wasn't insignificant either.

You may be called to make great sacrifices for things you believe in or you may not, but don't think that what you are doing today has to be grand and heroic in order to matter. Don't discount the value of beginning. The big change rarely comes out of the blue. It doesn't have to happen overnight. In fact, I don't know of a time when it ever has.

5

Heroes and Movements

Don't call me a saint. I don't want to be dismissed that easily.

—Dorothy Day

Growing up as a middle-class White kid in the seventies on the Gulf Coast of Florida, I had brown corduroy pants, a black-and-white TV in the living room, feathered hair, and a Trapper Keeper notebook. The widespread cultural turmoil of the civil rights era had subsided, and, other than the occasional school bully and a vague concern that nuclear annihilation might come any day, the cultural space I inhabited felt fairly calm and predictable.

I was born three weeks to the day after Martin Luther King, Jr. was killed. By the time I entered middle school, it had been a generation since Rosa Parks was arrested. Her story had seasoned sufficiently to feel safe for textbooks. Mrs. Parks was held up as a hero: a seemingly powerless little old African-American lady who had, the textbooks said, made a spontaneous decision not to relinquish her seat to a White man on a Montgomery bus in 1955 and literally changed the world through her courage.

I was inspired by her story, as I still am. But the shape of that inspiration has changed fundamentally. What I didn't know as a young student was that the version I was being taught had left out or glossed over much of the truth—those aspects of the story that I now believe to be some of the most important parts—and in some cases, it was simply incorrect.

To begin with, Rosa Parks was hardly a "little old lady." On December 1, 1955, the day of her arrest, she was forty-two years old. As I write these words, the age of forty-two is distant in my rearview mirror, and I sincerely hope that as you read this, you're offering a hearty "Amen!" that forty-two is not terribly old.

Of course, it may well be that as a young boy, I would have considered forty-two ancient. I'm not sure it has tremendous significance anyway, except that it seems to reinforce the perception of her spontaneous rise from helplessness to heroism.

There are other details that are interesting as well, like the fact that Mrs. Parks had Native American and White ancestry as well. Like my own grandmother, also named Rosa, she had long, wavy hair that she only let down at home, pinning it up in elaborate braids and buns whenever she left the house. Without doing anything at all, her very identity challenged the idea that "races" can be neatly categorized and separated.

> **Rosa Parks was not arrested for refusing to stand up so that a White man could have her seat.**

Many other facts are frequently left out of the story as well, removing painful details of the degrading, systematic oppression she and many others suffered. I won't spend a lot of time on them here, but it is worth mentioning that the central detail of Rosa Parks's famous arrest is generally told wrong.

There was not a White section and a Black section on buses in Montgomery in 1955, where each were free to sit. There was a White section (ten of the thirty-six seats), where people of color were not allowed to sit even if the rest of the bus was full and the White section was empty. The back ten seats were informally considered the "Colored" section, though there was no rule to designate them as such. The White section expanded as more Whites got on. A small sign indicating "Whites only" was moved back, row by row, and the people sitting in that row would need to rise and go stand at the back. The entire row would rise and stand, frequently leaving only one White person sitting in that row, alone.

That is exactly what happened on December 1, 1955. Rosa Parks was not arrested for refusing to stand up so that a White man could have her seat; she was arrested for refusing to stand so that a White man could have three empty seats beside him, sparing him the supposed indignity of sitting *across the aisle* from a Black woman, with two empty seats and an aisle between them.

I hope your anger rises a bit at that realization. The truth of that story, it turns out, is even more degrading than many of us were taught. There is, however, a much more important difference between the story I was told and the truth.

No one told me in grade school that by the time she was arrested, Rosa Parks had already been an activist for over two decades. Twelve years before that, she had become the secretary for the Montgomery chapter of the NAACP (National Association for the Advancement of Colored People), and she was involved in the Women's Political Council in Montgomery. She was a day-in, day-out activist for many years before the day that wrote her name in the history books and for decades afterward.

The summer before she was arrested, Rosa Parks had traveled to the Highlander Folk School in Tennessee for a workshop called "Racial Desegregation: Implementing the Supreme Court Decision," a reference to the *Brown v. Board of Education* ruling, which had been issued the year before. She spent ten days there taking classes and studying with legendary activists like Septima Clark and Myles Horton, a co-founder of Highlander. Highlander was a hub of civil rights training, voting rights activism, and other social action training in that era, and it was an extremely important part of the growing civil rights movement. It was at an informal Pete Seeger concert at Highlander that Dr. King first heard the song "We Shall Overcome".

Mrs. Parks writes in her autobiography, *My Story*, that her arrest that day was not premeditated, and that she did not set out to provide a test case for litigation. Nonetheless, she was very clearly prepared for this moment by her long years of activism and movement work. Her decision to defy the bus driver that day was not a spur-of-the-moment revelation or flash of courage, but rather the result of long-considered convictions and years of work, training, and practice. That changes the narrative of her famous stand (or rather, sit) in significant ways.

For most of us, Rosa Parks' life is one day long—December 1, 1955. But her arrest was hardly the first decision point in her journey. Nor was it the last.

This change in the story is extremely important. The two different versions of these events demonstrate the fundamentally different perspectives embedded in these two conflicting narratives about how large-scale social change happens. What's more, these two perspectives on the story give us very different sets of instructions for what to do if we would like to work for change.

I was first introduced to the discrepancies between the popular, sanitized version of Rosa Parks's first arrest and the more nuanced and complete story by author and activist Paul Loeb in his book *Soul of a Citizen*, and I have continued to learn more about it over the years since I encountered it there. Loeb points to this story as an excellent example of the lengths to which many people will go, consciously or subconsciously, to support the *Hero Narrative* of change.

> There is one problem with the Hero Narrative, however: it is not true.

In this narrative, large scale change happens when an extraordinary individual takes dramatic action in a moment of crisis. Then the problem is fixed, the threat is removed, and the credits roll. We love that storyline, as evidenced by the fact that it provides the plot for most of our entertainment, and arguably our history books as well.

There is one problem with the Hero Narrative, however: it is not true.

Of course, some people do heroic things. But heroes are seldom, if ever, the ones who effect change on a large scale.

That is admittedly a bold claim, and I intend to defend it. In order to do so, it may be useful to take a look at another hero story. On January 2, 2007, Wesley Autrey was on his way home from work in New York City, where he lives, waiting for a subway train with his two daughters, when a young man near him had an epileptic seizure and fell onto the tracks below. Autrey and another bystander jumped down onto the rails to try to pull him to safety. As they got there, they heard a train coming. The other person who had jumped down made the reasonable decision to clamber back up onto the platform. Autrey, however, eyed the space between the train and the gravel beneath it, then moved the young man into the space between the rails and covered him with his own body while several train cars raced over them. The space between the ground and the train was about twelve inches, and when the two were pulled up again, Autrey had grease on his hat from the bottom of the train.

There's no question that what Autrey did was profoundly heroic, self-sacrificing, and admirable. And his actions unquestionably had a big effect on Cameron Hollopeter, the young film student whom Autrey saved. It also warmed the hearts of a lot of other people, nationally and internationally. Autrey was all over the news and talk shows, and he received many gifts of gratitude from both anonymous and well-known benefactors.[10] In 2007 he was listed among *Time* magazine's "100 Most Influential People in the World." It is easy and appropriate to celebrate this man's courage.

And Wesley Autrey ticks all of the boxes for the Hero Narrative. If for no other reason, he can be considered a person of extraordinary courage based on this act alone. Few of us can imagine that we would have taken such a risk for a stranger. The dramatic act was in response to an unforeseen crisis, the threat was removed, and the problem was fixed. That's the Hero Narrative of change in technicolor.

But his story is not a very good model for large-scale change. Why not? Let's look at a competing narrative for how change happens.

The *Movement Narrative* says that large-scale social change is brought about by movements—many people taking small actions that contribute to a large shift. What Rosa Parks did is one such example. She was a daily activist, doing the work of a secretary with, I suspect, all the heroic drama and excitement that title invokes.

This daily activism continued to inform her choices, as did her experience working on a military base, where she first experienced a more integrated society. Together, these and other influences inspired her to delve deeper into social justice work, seek further training, and eventually take the dramatic stand that she took on that bus, as well as many other courageous choices that are largely unknown and

---

[10]Ellen Degeneres had Autrey on her show and gave him a Jeep Patriot. He was wearing a knitted hat with a Playboy logo on the day of his heroic action, and Playboy sent him another Jeep Patriot, and a lifetime subscription.

uncelebrated.

In short, Rosa Parks did not start with the action we all remember today. She started by getting involved in a small, undramatic way, and she continued to work in those ways for years before and after her moment of fame. She understood that the accumulated daily work she did throughout her life was what was most important, not the one action that made her famous.

The problem is that for most of us, heroic stories like Wesley Autrey's and the selectively edited version of Rosa Parks's—not to mention Dr. King's or Gandhi's—can be more immobilizing than encouraging. These kinds of heroes seem fundamentally different from us, dramatic and larger than life, so the idea of their action being a model for our own doesn't even occur to us. If we consider emulating them, we usually focus on the wrong part; we wonder whether we would have the courage to be arrested on that bus, rather than wondering whether we can clear the time to go to a meeting about an issue in our communities.

> The greatness of our heroes is not rooted in their fundamental nature, but in an accumulation of small, daily choices.

In fact, comparing ourselves to our heroes feels vaguely arrogant. Why? I think it's because of our internalization of the Hero Narrative. We have bought into the idea that they are a fundamentally different kind of people from us. We interpret this not just as a question of doing what they did, but of being *the kind of person* they were or are. To compare ourselves, therefore, is to inflate our own significance. We are normal and flawed. They are *übermenschen*, giants, saints.

That's wrongheaded. They are neither. The greatness of our heroes is not rooted in their fundamental nature, but in an accumulation of small, daily choices.

Paul Loeb articulates this well in *Soul of a Citizen: Living with Conviction in Challenging Times*:

> Chief among the obstacles to acting on these impulses [to work for change] is the mistaken belief that anyone who takes a committed public stand, or at least an effective one,

has to be a larger-than-life figure—someone with more time, energy, courage, vision or knowledge than a normal person could ever possess. This belief pervades our society, in part because the media tends not to represent heroism as the work of ordinary human beings, which it almost always is.

In this passage, Loeb echoes the famed Catholic Worker activist Dorothy Day's response to a young reporter who expressed his delight at the opportunity to speak with a saint. "Don't call me a saint," Day replied, "I don't want to be dismissed that easily." If we separate heroes from the rest of us, then their stories don't call us to action; they only call us to marvel and applaud. James Martin, S.J., the young man who interviewed her that day, later reflected on the conversation and wrote that she went on to say, "When they call you a saint it means basically that you are not to be taken seriously."

I suspect that most of the people who have been formally or informally sainted, and therefore separated from the rest of us, would consider such awe and separation to be the worst possible outcome of their notoriety. They would presumably prefer that we begin by taking on something small and getting involved, as each of them did, rather than be awed into immobility.

In an interview with the *New York Times*, Wesley Autrey said, "I don't feel like I did something spectacular; I just saw someone who needed help. I did what I felt was right." In his 2007 State of the Union Address, George W. Bush praised Autrey, saying "He insists he's not a hero."

Perhaps the denial of *being* a hero points back to how ingrained the hero myth is. Even the hero, in the moment when there is evidence of their heroic action, seems incapable of thinking of themselves as a hero. We know that heroes are "special" people, set apart, and we know that we are "normal" people with normal capacities. "I'm not a hero," our hero says, despite evidence to the contrary. "I'm just a normal person. I just did what I had to do."

It might make more sense to define heroes as "people who do heroic things," but that's not the definition we actually use. The idea that heroes are defined by their fundamental nature—their difference from the rest of us, their extraordinariness, rather than their choices and actions—is the first point in the definition of the Hero Narrative.

Implied in the denial of being a hero is this syllogism: "Heroes are special. I'm not special; I'm normal. Therefore, I'm not a hero."

We often follow that logic with more like it: "Heroes make a difference. I'm not a hero. Therefore, I can't make a difference."

But the problems with the Hero Narrative don't stop there. Even if you can imagine yourself as a hero, and we assume that heroism is what has a significant effect, how do you practice your heroism in order to effect change? Where will you find your oncoming train and student in distress?

This is the Hero Narrative, in a nutshell:

Things change when someone extraordinary responds to a moment of crisis with dramatic action.

This narrative has three elements: The first is that there is something inherently *special* about the hero. They are extra-ordinary, not ordinary. Perhaps the heroic person is extraordinarily courageous, like Wesley Autrey or Rosa Parks, or extremely smart, or persistent, or strong, etc.

The second is that there is a moment of *crisis* to which the hero responds. Here, crisis is an urgent danger that must be addressed in this moment, not tomorrow, or even ten minutes from now. The defining characteristic is not how big the problem is, but how urgent it is.

The third is that rather than taking ongoing, small, deliberative actions, the hero responds with *dramatic* action, making quick and extreme decisions in response to an urgent situation that arises without their agency.

I believe that most of us subconsciously subscribe to the Hero Narrative. And no wonder. The story is deep in our cultural context. It is the plot to many (perhaps most) of our movies. Movies with plots that center on movements, in which normal people work for change together in community with sustained but less dramatic action, are significantly harder to find.

In making the movie *Selma*, filmmaker Ava DuVernay fought to re-rewrite the script, which she said was originally written as a struggle between Dr. King and President Johnson, rather than a story of the people who drove the movement. "There was no way I could get my hands on this script called *Selma* about that time and not insert and assert the position, the point of view, the presence of Black people that were the actual people who did the work," DuVernay said. "Dr. King was an incredible strategist and mouthpiece for the movement. But the movement was people. It was those people who decided to boycott on the bus and not go to work." Though it met with broad critical acclaim and was nominated for two Academy Awards and four Golden Globes, some people criticized the film for not focusing sufficiently on King.

The fact that the Hero Narrative is deeply woven into our cultural consciousness combines with the fact that it is false and disempowering to create a dangerous and dysfunctional cultural force. If we draw guidance for our actions from the stories we consume about how the world works (and I believe we do), then this is one story we may need to reconsider.

Let me reiterate why. If we subscribe to the hero myth and we want to have a positive impact, then our instructions are essentially:

Step One: Wait for the crisis.

Wait and watch for the right moment, when the train is coming or the bus driver asks you to give up your seat, or someone external to you presents a situation that calls for courage and action.

This is a fundamental problem with the Hero Narrative: it is *reactive* rather than *proactive*. If the crisis never emerges, then you take no action.

The hero narrative makes no mention of the slow-moving systemic problems that do so much damage every day. It teaches that real change comes when you are confronted head-on with injustice and respond dramatically, and often violently.

But let's say that the crisis does emerge. Sometimes they do. Then what are your next instructions?

Step Two: Wait for the hero.

I suspect that there are very few of us who wake up in the morning feeling heroic, and walk through the world that way. As we have already discussed, we tend to see heroes as other people, special people, fundamentally different from ourselves. In the movies, they seem to show up when there is a crisis and they are needed.

When you read the story of Wesley Autrey's dramatic subway rescue, was your reaction, "That's probably what I would have done," or did it serve to reinforce the difference between you and heroes? We tell hero stories to inspire, but they can just as often disempower.

But even if you can find a hero, or you are among the few humans who could perceive *themselves* as a hero, then what are your next instructions?

Step Three:

There is seldom a step three because in the absence of proactive engagement, we end up waiting forever for the crisis and the hero to emerge. A very rare few of us may, like Wesley Autrey, find ourselves in a moment of crisis and summon the bravery to do something heroic, and that's wonderful. But is it a useful model for effecting systemic change?

I have nothing but respect for Wesley Autrey, but I question the effectiveness of this story as a template for positive change. If this is the pattern I want to emulate, then what should I do? Should I spend more time in subway stations waiting for someone to fall? If this is our model, then how do we deal with climate change, for instance? Should we hang out on icebergs and catch polar bears?

One significant problem with this model is that it denies agency; it emphasizes what happens to you and how you react, and de-emphasizes your ability to examine your situation and make intentional choices about how best to engage in the absence of a crisis.

Subscribing to the Hero Narrative of change can easily make us feel like a little boy at Halloween in his Superman costume, waiting on the porch for someone to cry out in distress so that he can save them. And waiting. And waiting. Finally, he gives up and goes to play some other game.

If, however, we subscribe to the movement model, then the instructions are quite different. They can be briefly summed up like this: Consider what you care about; where your deepest concern is right now. Find your community, learn from them, listen deeply to the people most directly affected. Build relationship. List the assets and tools that the group possesses. Lay out an achievable plan together to use those tools in the service of changes you wish to see. Begin by doing something small. Bite off a chewable piece and start chewing.

Those are very different instructions.

The Hero Narrative is so deeply ingrained in our cultural psyche that we often don't even realize it's there, and we've built quite a few castles on its bad foundation. I doubt that the various people who gradually edited Rosa Parks's story down till it fit the hero myth were doing so consciously. I suspect they were just trying to tell the story well and dramatically, so they made it conform to the narrative that heroes are extraordinary people who respond to a crisis with dramatic and unpremeditated action.

That myth also informed a clickbait article I read online a few years ago. The title of the article was rather cynical, and I should have resisted the temptation to open it, but my curiosity got the better of me. It was called, "The 8 Most Overrated People in History."

> Is the author seriously suggesting that to be a real hero Gandhi should have expelled the British Empire from India single-handedly?

M.K. Gandhi was on the list. Having studied Gandhi and worked in India with people who knew and worked with him, I found his inclusion intriguing and surprising.

Briefly put, the author's criticism was that, "[Gandhi] was a figurehead for the cause, while various other leaders were doing most of the work," and that, "the Indian independence movement was a strong force well before Gandhi entered the scene."

From one perspective, the author was not so far from the truth: Yes, a lot of others did most of the work in the Indian independence movement, and they had certainly done a lot of work before Gandhi became involved.

But is the author seriously suggesting that to be a real hero Gandhi should have expelled the British Empire from India single-handedly, and that he should have come up with a solution on the spot rather than building on the work of other activists? That's what the Hero Narrative would require. A *real* hero, a James Bond figure, would have taken care of the problem himself.

In the real world, effective leaders *invite others* to join them in their work, including those who will become the next generation of leaders. They do not keep the focus on themselves, as much as we try to put it there.

A hero story that inspires others to get involved can be useful in nourishing a movement, but it is more common for a hero story to keep the focus on the hero rather than the movement. It allows us to outsource good work, rather than showing up ourselves.

If we want to see positive change, the goal is to get a lot of people involved. And when a lot of people move a little bit, the problems begin to be addressed. This is the difference between a hero and a leader. The leader keeps the focus on the movement. The Hero Narrative teaches that the hero will make the change *for* us, rather than with us.

> The Hero Narrative teaches that the hero will make the change for us, rather than with us.

In the real world, however, heroes seldom, if ever, have significant impact on large scale problems in the absence of a movement. At their best, heroes inspire others to get involved and address the problem together. That's how things really change. So we can be grateful for the inspiration Gandhi provided, rather than being offended that he got too much attention.

What effect did Rosa Parks's arrest have? The arrest *on its own* meant little. Several others had been arrested in similar circumstances in Montgomery before her, notably Claudette Colvin. Rosa Parks's arrest had three huge and overarching effects, though, all of which were interwoven.

First, it provided a test case for the court system, *Browder v. Gale*, which was eventually won by Montgomery lawyer Fred Gray before the United States Supreme Court. Second, it served as the catalyst for a one-day bus boycott, which was so successful that it turned into a boycott that was kept up for over a year.

The third reason is perhaps the most important: Rosa Parks's arrest had a huge effect on public opinion, because it was widely publicized. By 1955, 64 percent of U.S. households had televisions. Here was a diminutive, dignified, well-dressed Black woman standing between two large White police officers, being arrested. We asked why. The clear answer was that she was being prosecuted for not giving up a seat on a public bus, despite having paid her fare.

Across the nation, there was a small shift. Many people were forced to examine and re-evaluate previously held assumptions about the inevitability and acceptability of "the way things are." It didn't fix the problem, but it did shift things slightly and significantly, and it fanned the flames of the civil rights movement in the United States.

Rosa Parks seemed to agree that her own action was not the most significant part of what happened that day. "At the time I was arrested I had no idea it would turn into this," she wrote. "It was just a day like any other day. The only thing that made it significant was that the masses of the people joined in."

> Movements don't need lots of leaders; they need lots of participants.

Leaders and heroes can be extremely important, but their importance lies in their ability to inspire and challenge the rest of us, not in their ability to directly right the wrongs. And the power that a leader holds is directly rooted in followers. The real power lies in movements—groups of people who are showing up to do their small part.

In fact, heroic figures and charismatic leaders are not always necessary for change, as demonstrated by the Egyptian chapter of the Arab Spring, in which a coalition of online and community activists overthrew the Mubarak regime through nonviolent resistance, with no one leader that we can hold up as the unifying figurehead. A leader without a movement is ineffectual in bringing about large-scale change. A movement without a charismatic, uniting leader is rare, but can still be effective.

One could make the counterargument that it is moneyed powers, not movements, that really change things. Certainly, it would be ridiculous to claim that top-down power and financial resources are not strong tools. Clearly, they are. They are not the only kinds of power, however;

and bottom-up, grassroots nonviolence can and often does defeat them, even in the face of formidable obstacles. Between 2000 and 2006 alone, organized nonviolent civilian movements successfully challenged entrenched power in Serbia, Madagascar, Georgia, Ukraine, Lebanon, and Nepal.

Even top-down power depends on the cooperation of the masses. Étienne de la Boétie, a young sixteenth-century political theorist, noted in a treatise he wrote as a law student that, "Obviously there is no need of fighting to overcome this single tyrant, for he is automatically defeated if the country refuses consent to its own enslavement." He has a point there, one that was picked up by many political theorists after him, including Robespierre and later the drafters of the United States Declaration of Independence. Top-down power is always predicated on bottom-up power. If well-organized and committed, the latter eventually wins.

Still, the Hero Narrative is deep in us, although it is demonstrably untrue. It informs many of the self-defeating voices in our heads, the ones that ask, "What difference could my tiny efforts make in the face of such a huge problem?"

In fact, those small efforts are the best shot we have at having a large impact. They are the most effective way to address a problem. Though the charge against such small actions is that they don't matter, it turns out that the exact opposite is true; they are the most pragmatic approach we can take.

If we cling to the myth that large scale change is effected by dramatic and heroic actions, we risk missing opportunities for real impact. As it turns out, movements are more effective than heroes. And movements don't need lots of leaders; they need lots of participants. In the end, the real power lies with us: normal people making small decisions to engage.

6

Small Change

We get to be a ripple in the water.

—The Indigo Girls, "Perfect World"

So we know what happened after Rosa Parks was arrested. The history books tell us that a group of pastors met the following evening at Dexter Avenue Baptist Church, and the Montgomery Improvement Association was formed four days later at Mt. Zion AME Church. They elected a young Rev. Dr. Martin Luther King, Jr., to be the president, apparently, as Rosa Parks wrote in her autobiography, because "he was so new to Montgomery and to civil rights work that he hadn't been there long enough to make any strong friends or enemies." We know that position launched him to national prominence and that these combined events ignited the civil rights movement (though, of course, that work had been going on for generations). We know that Rosa Parks became an icon of courage and that profound changes came to the United States in the wake of her actions.

Now I want to look in the other direction on the timeline of Mrs. Parks's life. As I mentioned before, she was trained in nonviolent activism at the Highlander Center the summer before she was first arrested in 1955. We know that she had worked for the Montgomery NAACP as its secretary since 1943. History also tells us that she married her husband Raymond Parks in 1935 and that he was already involved with anti-racism activism when they married.

For eight years, Raymond Parks went to organizing meetings about race issues, and Rosa Parks stayed home. Apparently, Raymond Parks discouraged his wife from going to NAACP meetings because he said it was too dangerous. When she finally did go, however, she quickly became involved, her stated reason for doing being a sign of the times; "I was the only woman there, and they said they needed a secretary," she wrote in her autobiography, "and I was too timid to say no."

I am glad she went to the meeting and glad she got further involved. I can't help but wonder, though, who invited Raymond Parks to *his* first meeting, and what that conversation might have sounded like. It is hard to imagine that he knew what history would unfold from that decision, and I wonder if the friend who invited him did so casually, or with intensity. The times were intense, but even in such times, with life or death issues to be addressed, our decisions to show up at a meeting or not can often hinge on who invites us and the mundanities of our weekly calendars and availability.

For Raymond and Rosa Parks, going to an NAACP meeting in Montgomery in 1935 was an entirely different proposition than going to one today. By going, they put their lives on the line. But I do find that even in the midst of dramatic and dangerous times, small details and casual human conversations are often hugely significant.

Looking at my own life, I can see corners on my own trajectory; times when I was headed one way but ended taking a turn in another direction, often due to a small influence. My decision to pursue music professionally, for instance, or meeting and later marrying my wife, or choosing to invite my son Mason into the world after wrestling for some time with whether we wanted to have children. Each of those decisions and so many others hinged on conversations and circumstances that seemed inconsequential at the time.

In the summer of 1987, I was working in Montreat, North Carolina, for the conference center there. In those days, the center hired about a hundred college students each summer to help run the place (it is many more than that now), and I was hired to run the audio-visual crew.

In my free time, I liked to hang around with some of the older staffers who had a band. The band changed names and personnel a bit each year, but that particular summer, Will Nash, Bill Graham, Patrick Miller, Nils Peterson, and sometimes Wade Powell made up the group. Even though I wasn't really a good enough guitar player to be in the band, they were kind enough to let me sit in on a song or two occasionally. I admired them all greatly, and I still do.

One night they let me play a few songs while they took their set break at the Town Pump, a local watering hole in Black Mountain. I plugged in my acoustic guitar, nervous but thrilled, and sang a James Taylor song and a couple of others.

While I was playing, Patrick, who was then finishing up a degree in classical guitar performance at the College of Wooster but also played a mean electric, wandered up to stand beside the stage and listen. When I finished my three songs, he cocked his head sideways so his unruly bangs were out of his eyes and said, "That was good, Dave. You could *do* this."

"Do what?"

"I mean, like, do *this*."

Looking back, I feel it seems like a rather low bar to have set; but at the time, I was blown away. Patrick, one of the best guitarists I had ever met, a guy who had the same relationship to cool that Midas had to gold, thought that I was a good enough guitar player and singer to play two-dollar-door gigs in smoky bars to the backs of people's heads while they watched a baseball game at the other end of the bar! To me, it sounded like a dream come true, and it was the first time I had seriously considered the possibility. I went home and did the math. How many shows would I have to do and what would I have to make to support a simple lifestyle?

Many years later, after my music career was established, interviewers have sometimes asked me when I knew I wanted to be a professional musician. I think that's the wrong question. If I ask a hundred fifteen-year-olds how many of them would like to have their life's work be making up songs and traveling the world to sing them for people, lots of hands will go up. Yet if I ask how many of them think that dream is possible for them personally, I get far fewer hands.

I know. Because I've done it.

The revelation for me wasn't that I wanted to do that, but that it might be possible. I had played guitar steadily for five years by the time

Patrick made that casual comment in the Town Pump, but for me it opened a door to a life that I hadn't thought was realistic. I still had to choose to go through the door and down the road, but that offhand comment pointed the way.

There are analogies to activism in that story. Many of us want to have a positive impact, but we don't get started because it doesn't occur to us that it is possible for us—specifically *you*, not 'people'—to have significant impact.

That story illustrates something else as well. It was such a casual comment for Patrick. I'm sure he didn't remember it a week later. Yet here I am more than three decades later, talking about it as a key moment in my life story. Certainly, there were many other influences that led me onto the path I've been walking, but that one mattered. Small efforts very often do.

> I am not arguing that all small changes lead to big ones. In my experience, some don't.

A cynic might respond by saying, "And they very often don't." That's true too, but it's irrelevant. I am not arguing that all small changes lead to big ones. In my experience, some don't. They just evaporate. But all big changes are made up of millions of small ones, many of which are determinative; the big change could not have happened without the little one.

One small effort can, and often does, have a huge effect, especially when it is combined with many other small efforts in the same direction. That leaves me passionate about the value of pursuing small changes, doing the simple things right in front of us. Inviting the friend to the meeting. Nudging someone down a path. Calling the governor's office to weigh in on a bill (and encouraging others to do the same). Getting a few friends together to talk about how we can have an impact on a given community issue that concerns us. Going to engage the people with whom you're having a problem. Making some copies of a flyer and posting them around town.

One of the most important small decisions we make, of course, is where we spend our money. If we are disturbed by the fact that much of our clothing is made by sweatshop labor, our twenty-first century form of slavery, then we can make the effort to search the Internet for which brands are "sweatshop free," buy more of our clothes at thrift shops, or simply buy fewer clothes.[11] If our college or faith community is printing up T-shirts for an event, we can buy them from a company that is committed to ethical labor practices. It's not terribly hard to find those folks, and though it may cost a bit more, it makes a huge difference in the lives of the people making those shirts.

My sister Kathy was a smoker for many years, and several attempts to quit had failed. In the end, the tipping point for her was her outrage at cigarette companies intentionally marketing to minors. She decided she simply could not give those companies any more of her money. Where we spend our money is sometimes a small decision, but small decisions add up.

It's the same with investments. It doesn't make sense to let a company borrow money from you to do things to which you object. There are investment brokers who specialize in responsible investing and can customize your portfolio to align with the issues you care about if you own stock.

But the deepest work, the work where we are transformed ourselves, is relational. In late 2019, my activist friend Holly Roach-Knight was part of a group of church folks in Asheville trying to develop networks of support for asylum seekers.

People who were fleeing violence in their home countries were coming to the United States border and presenting themselves to border officials to be given asylum, in keeping with several international treaties to which the United States has committed. They were not breaking laws, but if they did not have family or other contacts who were willing to take them in and sign documents to take some responsibility for supporting them, they were often detained (incarcerated) while they waited for their court dates. This is still the case.

It seemed to me that my small town, Black Mountain, had the resources to support a family, and there were enough people willing to do the work, so I called a meeting at our local music venue, the White Horse, and quietly invited everyone I knew in local faith communities and

[11]For more information on sweatshop free products, visit sweatfree-shop.com.

various other groups who might be sympathetic. Instead of making formal requests for support to the churches themselves, I asked individual people I knew in each church, and some folks who were not affiliated with faith communities, anyone who might be interested in this work. I invited them to come out for a conversation about supporting a family.

Over forty people came out, in a town of about nine thousand, and after a song from me and an introduction to the issue by Holly, we asked if folks were ready to take this on and if so, what role they might play in the effort. My friend Susan Murty agreed to help me lead the group, and another friend, Marshall Baltazar, later joined us.

That first night, the feeling of possibility in the room was truly exciting. People who were deeply troubled by this situation now had a way to contribute tangibly to making it better for one family. We had set the room with a horseshoe of chairs, so that we could focus on each other as well as the front of the room where people were sometimes presenting. This room setup contributed to the general sense of camaraderie.

Around the outside of that horseshoe, we had put large pieces of newsprint on small tables, each with a big topic on it—transportation, translation and interpretation, educational assistance, housing, hospitality, fundraising, etc. We introduced the areas in which folks would need assistance and then invited people to go to the table in keeping with their own gifts and passions. Once there, people introduced themselves, wrote their contact information on the newsprint, chose a convener for their task group, and started to brainstorm and do an asset inventory—who had what to contribute.

By the end of the night, we had a small organizational structure and options for lodging, a team of interpreters with an impressive list of languages they could cover, a great transportation team, and a host of other resources, including a place for the family to live.

Within a couple of weeks, we got word that there was a single mother with four children who needed a place to be; and we had teams ready to receive them, give them a safe and quiet place to land, and start to learn about what they needed to heal and move forward. It was a truly beautiful and empowering experience.

To say that it was beautiful is not to say that it was easy. Not long after their arrival, the whole country went into lockdown due to the COVID-19 pandemic, and this made everything more difficult. After a few months, the family decided that they needed to return to Mexico. Asylum cases are extremely difficult to win, and immigration officials had made it very clear that their chances were vanishingly small. Still, the family felt loved and supported while they were here, and they were not in detention when the pandemic hit, a situation that turned out to be fatal for some detainees.

In retrospect, I think the key to that team working well together was that many people were each making reasonable commitments. We could create this space because there were lots of us, and because people were bringing the part they had to bring. It was not a hero story, it was a movement story.

We also got to know each other and built relationships not only with the family that had come to stay, but among folks who had lived in the same town for years but hadn't known each other well or at all. Those relationships and organizational lessons have served us well in the years since, and we continue to learn as we make room in the community for more immigrant families in need. That work has also raised important questions about how we are caring for each other in the community when it comes to families who have been here for years and do not have what they need to get by. If we can mobilize for newcomers fleeing a dangerous situation, can we do the same for neighbors who are already here?

You may make small efforts to resist (or at least refuse to support) something to which you object, or you may make positive efforts to support something in which you do believe. In both cases, the small change can be hugely significant. The illustrations for this are as myriad as the people doing the work, but one of my favorites is the story of Jo Ann Robinson, another hero of the Montgomery bus boycott, but one whose name we hear much less than Rosa Parks.

Mrs. Parks was arrested on a Thursday evening on her way home from work. The news spread quickly through the Black community, and that evening, attorney Fred Gray and civil rights legend E.D. Nixon both talked with Jo Ann Robinson, discussing Mrs. Parks's arrest and how the movement could best respond. Jo Ann Robinson was the

President of the Women's Political Council, an organization of Black women working toward racial equity in Montgomery.

After those conversations with other Montgomery civil rights leaders, Ms. Robinson decided that the Women's Political Council should call for a one-day bus boycott. By midnight, she and two of the students she taught at Alabama State University were printing flyers. On an old school mimeograph machine, they ran 17,500 copies of a flyer calling for Montgomery's Black community to stay off of the buses on Monday.

Ms. Robinson and the students ran copies until 4 a.m. and then delivered them around town until 7 a.m.; then she went to teach her 8 a.m. class. The flyers were spread all over town through the network of the Montgomery Women's Political Council. Local ministers had a meeting on Friday morning and got behind the boycott as well. In church on Sunday morning, the Black community was again informed of the boycott and encouraged to participate.

> Rosa Parks's arrest provided the catalyst, but the plans and the framework had been in place for more than a year.

As important as that all-night printing sprint was, it was simply another chapter in the work Jo Ann Robinson had been doing for years as a leader in the Women's Political Council of Montgomery. The Council had three chapters and had built networks that provided structure for organizing the boycott once the decision was made. Rosa Parks's arrest provided the catalyst, but the plans and the framework had been in place for more than a year. Without that advance preparation, it is hard to imagine that the boycott could have been so successful. There was likely very little that could be considered dramatic in that behind-the-scenes work. Many meetings were held, and decisions were made together by many, many people whose small contributions have been forgotten. But they were essential.

Having asked hundreds of audiences to raise their hands if they have ever heard of Jo Ann Robinson or the Women's Political Council, I have found that almost no one has. Jo Ann Robinson called the Montgomery Bus Boycott, and the Women's Political Council organized it, but we seldom tell movement stories.

The problems we face as communities, as a nation, and as a world are indeed daunting. But it might be wise to scale down our thinking, at least at first, so that we can act, rather than being overwhelmed and immobilized. Rosa Parks didn't decide to go to jail in 1943. She decided to go to a meeting. Then she decided to help out. Even before her arrest, her work was essential to the movement, just as the work of Jo Ann Robinson and the Women's Political Council was. And what of the two students who helped run those copies? They occupy a significant place in history, but I can't find their names written down anywhere. All we know is that they were students who were enrolled in the class Jo Ann Robinson taught that Friday morning.

But there's more. Not only did Rosa Parks do years of day-to-day work for the cause *before* she was arrested, she immediately went back to that work afterwards. Many people will recognize a famous photograph of her being fingerprinted. When I search the internet for "Rosa Parks arrest," it is the first image that comes up on the screen. But that photograph is not from her famous arrest on December 1, 1955, but from a subsequent arrest in February, 1956, when 115 boycott leaders were arrested after the boycott was deemed illegal

Rosa Parks's second arrest, February 22, 1956.   AP Photo/Gene Herrick

under an arcane Alabama law against conducting an unjustified boycott.

The boycott came down to so much more than simply not riding the bus, and many people were involved in keeping it sustainable. People who were forgoing the buses still had to get to work and other places, so the organizers of the boycott purchased and accepted donations of six station wagons. They also organized 325 private citizens to help with transportation and worked with the local Black taxis to ensure that everyone had a ride to work. Mrs. Parks volunteered as a dispatcher, answering the phone and organizing pick-ups and drop-offs for boycotters. This famous photograph records her arrest for that work, not her better-known arrest for civil disobedience.

The moral of this story is not that the day-to-day work she had done before her arrest mattered because it led her to that famous moment on the bus, which *really* mattered. Rosa Parks understood that her most important work *was* the day-to-day work she did rather than the much-publicized moment for which she is remembered. She put most of her energy into that work for years before and after her celebrated arrest.

It is easy to be immobilized by the enormity of problems we face. We sit still because we can't imagine doing anything on a large enough scale to have a meaningful impact. We think that large problems demand large efforts at correction, and that's true. But we forget that those large efforts are almost always made up of millions of small efforts. Perhaps *your* small contribution is essential for a large-scale change.

7

The Flawed Hero

The sailor cannot see the north, but knows the needle can.

—Emily Dickinson

September 16, 2011I'm writing today in a setting that is strange for me: a roomy seat in the first class cabin of a US Airways flight to Dallas, Texas. I'll be performing tonight and speaking tomorrow in the towns of Edom and Tyler, and I'm looking forward to that time. Though I've been traveling almost constantly for more than twenty years now and have seen a great deal of the planet, I think this is only the second time in my life that I've flown first class.

Today's luxury is due to an airline pricing anomaly. Because I have to fly with my guitar, pedal box, and various other bits of gear, I need to check two bags. The airline was offering an upgrade special for one hundred dollars, which means it was cheaper to buy the upgrade than to pay for my baggage. Life is pretty good up here, though the flight attendant clearly spots me as a stranger and kindly keeps explaining things to me.

As I loaded my guitar and suitcase into the car this morning in Chapel Hill, a light rain was falling. I was grateful for my Aussie hat and a hand-me-down rain jacket that had once belonged to my wife, Deanna. We sent it to the thrift shop when she no longer needed it, and my mother bought it for me later, not knowing that Deanna had once owned it. It serves me well, and I'm glad it came back to us.

This morning was cool and gray, uncharacteristically early in the season for that kind of weather in central North Carolina, and if I had said, "What a beautiful sunny day!" to my son Mason, it would doubtless have confirmed some of his concerns about his dad's mental stability; it was clearly grim and drizzly. I often think that this is how many people perceive peace activists—somewhat delusional, living in some Pollyanna world where black is white, rain is sun, and despair is hope.

As our plane took off, though, we bumped up through the clouds, and suddenly there was bright sunshine and blue sky. The plane was more or less right above the house we rent in Chapel Hill when it broke through the clouds, and there it was: a clear, sunny day. That sight is shocking after the weighty gray of the morning. I'm still looking out the window at that sunshine now.

> We love to picture our heroes as people without flaws, and then, when we inevitably discover that they do have flaws, we love to tear them down again.

It doesn't make the rain a lie. It's still a soggy day at my house; I got soaked packing the car. But the sunshine isn't a lie either, and I haven't traveled very far. Both are true; both are present and real, though only one was visible from my driveway.

It is easy to fall into Manichaean thought—either/or dichotomies—and it is common to apply such thought to heroes. We love to picture our heroes as people without flaws, and then, when we inevitably discover that they *do* have flaws, we love to tear them down again.

As people with firsthand experience of what it means to be human beings, it seems as if we ought to have a bit more insight than that. Our own decision-making is flawed, and our self-centered natures are certainly manifest, but that doesn't mean we don't have noble motivations as well. As it turns out, all of our motivations are mixed, and all of us are complicated creatures.

Human purity is virtually unknown, and I tend to believe it's overrated as a goal in the first place. I am all in favor of aiming for growth, but purity is unachievable, and over-emphasizing it sets us up for failure. The problem, conceptually and practically, is that because we assign purity to some individuals and not others, we have the capacity to do two things. The first I discussed in the previous chapter: We can categorize some people—"heroes"—as fundamentally different from ourselves by stripping them of their human frailty. We can't be motivated by their examples, we reason, because we can't compare ourselves to such noble beings. We then excuse ourselves from any responsibility for action because we deny any similarity between our heroes and ourselves. It is virtually impossible to relate to their moral purity and what seems to be their inevitable destiny for greatness.

Given that tendency, once their moral flaws and incapacities are revealed, we might expect that we would reconsider that fundamental difference between ourselves and our heroes, and perhaps wonder if we, flawed as we are, might be called to take positive action as well. Unfortunately, that's usually not the way it goes.

> I have often heard people say, "World peace begins by finding peace within oneself." But while peace may begin there, it certainly doesn't end there.

Instead, we switch to the second problem with lionizing our heroes: once their frailties and failures are exposed, we dismiss their efforts as hypocritical and disparage any good they might have done. We point to Dr. King's alleged affairs or Gandhi's legendary temper and say, "Some peacemakers *they* were!"

That reasoning also allows us to sit on the sidelines once more, since those do-gooders seem to be up to no good after all. "They're all a bunch of hypocrites and charlatans!" we say. "What's the point?" We might even go further and argue that all people are fundamentally malicious and self-serving, as our broken heroes demonstrate. And if people are fundamentally broken, then why should we try to make any sort of change for good?

So we have it both ways and manage to get ourselves off the hook by switching our logic midstream. Whether we see our heroes as perfect or flawed, we have developed easy rationalizations to excuse ourselves from any kind of responsibility to join them in their work or to take up work of our own.

I don't think it's that simple. The truth isn't that human nature is fundamentally good and altruistic, nor that it is fundamentally selfish and evil. We are neither good nor bad; we are multifaceted and malleable. Russian novelist and dissident Aleksandr Solzhenitsyn got it right when he said, "The line dividing good and evil cuts through the heart of every human being."

Years ago when I wrote the journal entry above, my son still lived in a world of good guys and bad guys, which was developmentally appropriate. As we grow older, however, we need to move past that paradigm, and many of us fail to do so. The result is often that we refrain from addressing problems we see; keenly aware of our own failings, we think they disqualify us from acting.

We don't have to wait until we are pure before we act. We can act now, imperfectly. We can honor the imperfection of the efforts of those around us and stop wasting precious energy on judgment, of them and of ourselves.

I have often heard people say, "World peace begins by finding peace within oneself." There is undoubtedly some truth to that. I have known people who identify as peacemakers who throw shrapnel everywhere they go, usually thwarting their own aims because of it. But while peace may begin there, it certainly doesn't end there. If we wait to be outwardly active until we are inwardly self-actualized, we will wait forever. It is as foolish to hold ourselves to standards of perfection as it is to hold our heroes to them. It may make more sense to do the inner work and the outer work at the same time, letting each inform the other, and bringing our imperfection to the work at hand.

As for me, I have a confession to make: I could get used to flying first class.

8

Paved with Good Intentions

The line dividing good and evil cuts through the heart of every human being.

—Aleksandr Solzhenitsyn

The first time that I flew first class, ironically, was on a trip to Guatemala to work with PEG Partners in extremely impoverished communities. I got bumped up on a full flight on my way to spend time in homes with dirt floors and limited access to clean water. Just in case my own privileged status in the world wasn't made clear enough to me on that trip, the hot towels and real glass for my drink certainly drew the line starkly.

There I was, sitting in a chair in the middle of the sky, suspended in a painful irony. I could have congratulated myself, I suppose, on spending my time and energy doing this work by which I hope to improve the chances of some underprivileged kids. I didn't have to be there, and that time is costly to me in significant ways.

But I was making that trip by spending not only financial resources, but natural resources as well. Air travel is one of the more destructive habits of the wealthier percentiles of the planet's population, and the money and carbon spent on that plane ticket could arguably have been spent for a better purpose than physically moving me back and forth.

I certainly gain a lot by going to Guatemala, too. I have made good friends there, and I enjoy the food and the company and the sometimes breathtaking beauty of the place. I try to make a couple of trips each year to Guatemala, and in the nearly twenty years since my wife, Deanna, and I founded this non-profit organization, I have spent a great deal of time running the part of it that happens back in the United States. I'm not paid for that work, but the organization does pay for part of my travel expenses, allowing me to spend time with friends in Guatemala without having to shoulder the entire financial burden myself.

It's good and healthy for me to have the chance to step away from my "normal" life in order to be reminded of how far from normal it seems to much of the world. There are many definitions of "'normal," and I need to be reminded of that occasionally in order to have a sense of who I am and where I fit into the world. Among the many reasons I am grateful for that time in Guatemala is that the occasional shift in perspective helps me understand my responsibilities—what is mine to do.

So this is volunteer work, and I clearly see the positive impact it has had for others for nearly twenty years. But I also enjoy it, and it's good for me, and sometimes fun. From time to time, I have to check in with myself about my motivations: Is this self-serving? Is my work in Guatemala a costly exercise in self-congratulation for a privileged do-gooder that ultimately has little real positive impact? Or is it a meaningful contribution? Is it a sacrifice or another privilege in a privileged life?

Is it worthwhile to develop those relationships and work on those very real justice issues in Guatemala, helping to open doors of opportunity for kids there who might not have much of a chance otherwise, and opening myself to challenging perceptions of where I fit into the problems? Is it a responsible action for a U.S. citizen to take, given my own country's role in manipulating governments and perpetuating inequality in Central America for our own economic gain?[12] Is it the best use of my time, passion, and energy to get involved in Guatemala when there are plenty of pressing needs in my own community in North Carolina? Those are questions with which I've wrestled for years, and I think it is important to keep wrestling with them because the balance may shift, and I certainly have much more to learn.

[12]For some context on U.S-Guatemala history, I recommend the book *Bitter Fruit: The Story of the American Coup in Guatemala*, by Stephen Schlesinger and Stephen Kinzer.

My working hypothesis is that it's both. I do believe that the positive impact we're having in Guatemala is significant and worthwhile. Through partnerships with other excellent organizations like FUNDIT, Child-Aid, and LEAF International, we are reaching thousands of Guatemalan children and facilitating not just literacy but also critical thinking skills, access to music and arts, cultural preservation, and mentoring from healthy and compassionate guides in their own communities. We are also nourishing local leaders who provide powerful examples for children in their own communities. "All of the projects are run by local leaders, with support from PEG.

Literacy, arts, and critical thinking are contributing factors for all of the changes that my Guatemalan friends tell me are needed in their country—political, economic, and social. If someone doubts that we're having a positive impact, I can introduce them to children whose lives are different, and arguably much better, because of our work. These kids will have more opportunities and more choices because of the higher quality of education and the significantly improved nutrition they are getting because they have a chance to go to school.

I once gave a talk about PEG's work, and during the question-and-response session that followed someone asked, "Why do you work overseas when there are so many problems right here in the United States? Isn't it easier to go somewhere else than to work in your own community?"

That is a common question and criticism, but I find it troubling for several reasons. First, it assumes that we can only do one or the other. It's a scarcity mentality. I think both are deeply important, and we are not limited to choosing one. Along with my work in Guatemala, I also work on issues in my own country, in my home state of North Carolina, and in my little town of Black Mountain. I absolutely believe that all of this work matters.

What disturbs me more is an undercurrent I sometimes perceive in that kind of question. If the questioner is saying, "Kids in our community matter too," then I wholeheartedly agree with that statement, and I encourage the person asking the question to work hard for kids in that community, since they bring that passion.

Sometimes, though, I get the feeling that the person asking that question is suggesting that kids in their community matter *more* than kids in other places. Those values are not unusual, but I do not share them. The late health care activist, doctor, and author Paul Farmer said, "The idea that some lives matter less is the root of all that is wrong with the world." That has a ring of truth to me.

The suggestion that it is easier to work outside the United States than it is to work in our own communities troubles me, too. In some ways it *can* be easier, especially if we do it poorly—if we don't maintain the relationships we form, instead parachuting in without long-term connection; if we impose our own solutions rather than listening and being guided and instructed by the people who are most directly affected; or if we travel like tourists and don't engage at a more personal level. Accountability, openness, and listening are fundamental to effective community.

In other ways, however, working in another country is harder. Time away from family, expense, getting out of one's cultural comfort zone, and sometimes real risk to personal safety are all part of the equation. I work in Guatemala for many reasons, including a sense of indebtedness for my government's destructive role in Guatemala's history, the fact that we can leverage so much impact with much smaller financial investment, and the degree of need, which is quite extreme. Mostly, though, we are there because friends there asked me to help. They had some of the pieces, and I had others, and together we have been able to do good things.

The PEG team has tried to learn from mentors, to study, to listen deeply, and to engage in long-term, committed relationships where everyone is bringing what they have, asking for what they need, and working together to create positive impact.

But there are also valid criticisms to be made. A good friend of mine believes that unless charity also engages in justice work, it is destructive because it props up untenable and unjust systems. She's seen it play out in her own community.

That friend, whom I'll call Jen, attended a church in a small southern town while she worked during the week as a community organizer and the director of a food bank. Many members of that church supported the food bank, where the poor residents of the town, primarily African Americans, often came to eat. Jen's church, made up primarily of middle- and upper-class White people, felt good about its charity, and the poor people in town had food that they needed, though presumably they may not have felt as good about the situation, trading dignity for food.

Most of the people who ate at the food bank worked at the mills in town, which were owned by some of the very people with whom Jen went to church. After she had been there some time, she found herself privy to conversations in which the mill owners complained about government regulations requiring them to improve ventilation in the mill to make it safe for the workers, and ways they were trying to get around those regulations to avoid the cost. "In addition," she told me, "People from my church owned loan companies that charged 25 percent interest, keeping people perennially in debt. They donated their used clothes, leftover food, and some money to charity, but they resisted any challenge to the system that perpetuated that poverty."

Over time, Jen came to understand that keeping the mill workers fed at the food bank was maintaining a system of abuse by a company that chose not to pay them enough to eat. They were replacing justice with charity. The soup kitchen was an enabler in this system as well as a salve to the consciences of her fellow parishioners, and Jen began to feel complicit in this system of abuse.

Back in Guatemala, helping to support public education efforts financially may make the Guatemalan government less willing to shoulder that responsibility itself. Or at least, like the mill owners at Jen's church, PEG Partners may help me and others sleep better at night in the face of the many global economic injustices in which we are participating.

Those are important and serious things to consider, and should not be lightly dismissed. Recall that aid work is trying to meet people's needs, while social justice work is challenging the systems that make them needy. And though I wish it were not true, I do believe that aid work can sometimes undercut justice work. Put otherwise, meeting people's short-term needs can undermine or retard systemic changes.

"Right now, I'm seeing more charity and mission trips than I have ever seen," Jen wrote to me. "And yet it is rare that these same people question why the charity is needed and what long term change they want to impact. For many of these folks, charity is the end of the line, and the only outcome they think is necessary." Speaking again of the relationship between the food bank and the church, she wrote, "The charity dulled everyone to the injustice of that whole economic system. The people in that church remained adamantly opposed to any and all social justice work."

Jen's growing understanding of the generationally entrenched injustice in her community eventually led her to leave that work and turn her attention to more systemic change, with which she is still involved. She remains understandably skeptical of charity.

The books *Toxic Charity* and *When Helping Hurts* both take on various ways in which well-intentioned aid projects can be destructive of dignity, relationships, and opportunities for larger shifts in oppressive systems. Those are important conversations to have, and though I have criticisms of each book, I think both of them offer good and useful insights.

> For many of these folks, charity is the end of the line, and the only outcome they think is necessary.

It seems to me, however, that there are also risks to overgeneralizing and dismissing all aid work as destructive. There are times when a short-term solution (aid) is needed to get through a crisis, so that we can find our way to a long-term shift toward sustainability and equity (justice).

I include Jen's story because it is real and relevant. Hope cannot be predicated on denying hard realities. But there is a danger in overextending the criticism of aid work. I also think it is important to acknowledge that not all aid work conforms to this pattern. We should be careful that valid critiques of charity do not simply end up as rationalization for withdrawing support of projects that could be improved, rather than doing the work of improving them, where that is a tenable possibility.

To return to the fable about aid v. social justice earlier in this book, marching the whole team upstream to see who is throwing the babies in the river means that the ones who are coming down now will likely drown. Ignoring justice work is self-defeating, as the story illustrates, but if we stop all aid work in favor of justice work, many people will suffer who did not have to.

In the context of PEG's work in Guatemala, it does not seem wise to sacrifice the education of this generation of children in order to keep up pressure on the government; certainly not when I'm asked to help and I have a way to do so. I think it is more likely that facilitating education, mentoring, and some training in critical thought will allow these children to grow up to challenge injustices in their own society than it is that our work will contribute to maintaining the status quo.

When we are challenging a flawed model, it's important to ask whether we are challenging it for the purpose of improving it or because it should be discarded. When we see that something is broken, we have the choice to ask, "How can we make it work better?" or to throw up our hands and say, "It's no use!" Sometimes it really is no use, and we should put our energy elsewhere. But if we give up on aid work on principle, we'll be throwing a lot of babies out with the river water.

> Ignoring justice work is self-defeating, as the story illustrates, but if we stop all aid work in favor of justice work, many people will suffer who did not have to.

In addition to the criticism that aid work can undercut justice work, it is often criticized as self-serving. The first critique is a question of outcomes, and the second is largely a question of motivation.

Taking my own inventory, I have no question that I feel good about my work with PEG Partners in Guatemala, and that is a benefit for me. So is that primarily why I do it? I can't deny that it is a factor. Of course, I want to feel as if I'm having a positive impact, and our work in Guatemala does give me some evidence that I am. I don't think it is the primary reason I'm doing this work, but I can't pretend that it isn't a part of the mix.

There are no absolutes in these conversations. If we remove the nuance, we remove part of the truth. The bottom line for me, though, is that all of our efforts as human beings are driven by complicated motivations and have mixed outcomes. We fail not by having impurity within us, but by valuing only purity. If we are to do what is needed, it might be wise for us to spend a bit less energy tearing down our own good efforts and each other's. Imperfect plans and mixed motivations can reach a point where they are problematic, but I strongly suggest that they are seldom our biggest problem. Apathy and inaction are of far greater concern, and attacking the motivation of good efforts is perhaps our most popular method for justifying our own inaction. Doing good work in the real world is messy and complicated, morally as well as practically.

The danger of moral absolutism is that it is yet another way to immobilize ourselves and each other. Ironically, the issues with the work become an excuse not to act, rather than a reason to address those imperfections, simply dismissing the people involved as hypocrites.

> Attacking the motivation of good efforts is perhaps our most popular method for justifying our own inaction.

If hypocrisy means that our actions sometimes fail to live up to our values, then we are all hypocrites. The question is whether we will be hypocrites who make the world a bit better today or hypocrites who spend our time calling each other hypocrites in order to justify our own refusal to get involved.

Hypocrisy sometimes has another definition, though. The word 'hypocrite' comes from the Greek, *hupokrisis*, which had to do with theatrical acting, or pretending. So there's an argument to be made that hypocrisy, at its core, doesn't really mean "not practicing what you preach," but "not *believing* what you preach." That's a more serious accusation.

A great deal of ink and air have been spent discussing the fundamental nature of humanity, whether we are essentially good or essentially evil—or perhaps, to put it differently, essentially selfish or essentially cooperative. But this conversation itself can paralyze us. We have the capacity for tremendous good and tremendous harm, for unfathomable generosity and self-sacrifice and for staggering selfishness and cruelty. Most of the time, though, we live neither on one end of the spectrum nor the other. We are a complicated mix of all of it, all in the same moment. And that is as true of our efforts in community as it is of our individual lives.

Outcomes, though they are somewhat more tangible than motivations, are still difficult to categorize. "First, do no harm," is a popular mantra among many people working for positive change, and a core tenet of the Hippocratic oath. I don't think it is a realistic promise, though. Sometimes even the most successful efforts simultaneously do real harm.

The United States civil rights movement, for example, decimated certain black-owned businesses. Between 1960 and 1980, the number of personal-service businesses owned by minorities decreased by 49.1 percent." African Americans were finally allowed to shop at businesses that were previously only available to Whites, but White customers did not support Black-owned businesses in the same way or to the same degree. Black children began to attend schools that were formally limited to White students but more than 38,000 black teachers lost their jobs after the Brown v. Board of Education ruling. That's not a reason to regret the movement or its achievements, however. It is an invitation to work on the next issues, some of which may arise from the good work that has been done, and to learn from history as we try to do better in our current efforts.

> "First, do no harm," is a popular mantra among many people working for positive change, and a core tenet of the Hippocratic oath. I don't think it is a realistic promise, though.

We cannot be cavalier about harm done, nor can we minimize it; but we should also not delude ourselves that any large-scale change can take place without some real harm. That can easily become one more way to paralyze ourselves.

In any effort for positive change, it is wise to study, plan, consult mentors, and reflect on earlier experience in order to minimize negative consequences. Crucially, people of privilege need to be guided and taught by people most directly affected. Together, we should try hard to maximize positive impact and minimize damage. All too often, though, we see complexity and simply quit before we begin, citing the downsides of something as though this is a rational argument for taking no action.

Good work is complicated and may cause damage, but inaction in the face of manifest injustice is simply opting for the harm we know rather than the potential for harm that we can't fully predict, thereby dismissing the possibility of improving the situation.

As it turns out, the adage is true: the road to hell *is* paved with good intentions. But the roads to compassion, community, and positive change are paved with the same stones, carefully laid by people who take the time to reflect about the final destination and how they intend to get there. The question is: Which road will we build?

9

Movement in the Wrong Direction

We can destroy ourselves with cynicism and disillusion just as effectively as by bombs.

—Kenneth Clark

On Valentine's Eve, 2015, Deanna and Mason and I packed up the car and drove four hours over to our state capitol, Raleigh, for the annual Historic Thousands on Jones Street march the next day. The HK on J rally, as it is known locally, is hosted by a coalition of different organizations that gather each year to petition the state legislature, located on Jones Street, on several pressing justice issues. We stayed with my former boss at the NC Council of Churches, George Reed, and his wife Susan, who have been like extra grandparents for Mason since we first got to know them.

With lots of time to kill in the car, we talked with Mason, then six years old, about what we were going to do and why. He has always been inquisitive, and he asked good questions. We talked about the issues being addressed by HK on J that year and explained why it is important to let our representatives know how we feel about those issues. We reminded him that sometimes people make signs at marches like this to tell people what they care most about or what they want the legislators to do. We talked a bit about clever signs we have seen at similar events and ideas for signs we might make. Mason was very interested in this conversation, and he seemed to be thinking hard about what he might put on a sign if he were to make one.

Eventually, we pulled into George and Susan's driveway and, after settling in a bit, we turned our conversation to the march. We told them that Mason wanted to make a sign and wondered whether they had some cardboard we could scavenge. It turned out that Susan had some actual poster board, and she took Mason into the next room to get some things for him to use. They came back a little while later, and Mason showed us his sign, which Susan insisted he made all by himself, taped to an old wooden ruler with George and Susan's son's name on the back. In a first-grader's handwriting, it read "evreewun is eekwl!"

Mason made that sign because, even at six, he was upset that our

Mason's message for the North Carolina legislature

leaders in the North Carolina legislature would make policies that devalue some people's welfare and dignity, and this was the thing he wanted to say to his representatives. We drove from western North Carolina to Raleigh and spent a chilly day in the streets because it felt important to us; and it did to him, too. Our investment was gas, food, and a couple of days' time. Not very large, in the context of sacrifices activists sometimes make, but a drop that helped to fill the proverbial bucket of Jones Street. That's part of what a movement looks like.

It was important to us that Mason, growing up in a time, place, and body that would make it easy for him to be unaware of the struggles of people around him, have a sense of those struggles and understand both the obligation to work for a better way, and the beautiful sense of solidarity one feels in a crowd of thousands of people who share that commitment. A few years earlier, when he was two, we took him to his first street protest in a stroller on Martin Luther King, Jr., Day, and he held the end of a stick with a printed picture of Dr. King that was given to us by organizers when we arrived. I held the other end, and we carried the sign together.

Saul Alinsky's most famous book, *Rules For Radicals*, has become an organizing manual for agitators and strategists across the political spectrum. On the first page of that book, he wrote, "*The Prince* was written by Machiavelli for the Haves on how to hold power. *Rules for Radicals* is written for the Have-Nots on how to take it away." *The Prince* was written in the sixteenth century as a guidebook for rulers. It justifies nearly any means available to them to maintain their power. Alinsky is making the assumption here, as I admit that I often have too, that movements represent the people in struggles against those authoritarian rulers. Looking through that dichotomous lens, my own sympathies naturally run to movements. But not all movements are created equal.

Astroturf – the accusation and the reality

When Justice Brett Kavanaugh was going through the confirmation process to become a Supreme Court judge in late 2018, protestors filled the streets each day, questioning his character after hearing testimony about his alleged sexual abuse and warning of the consequences of naming him to the Supreme Court, due to his judicial record. The protests were large, vociferous, and passionate, and the population of the United States was predictably divided on the question.

Then-President Trump's response to these demonstrations was to insult the protestors in a very particular way; he wrote, via Twitter, "look at all of the professionally made identical signs. Paid for by Soros and others. These are not signs made in the basement from love!" (For the record, my family's belief in the causes for which we showed up and marched in Raleigh was just as sincere when we carried a pre-printed sign as when Mason made his own sign "in the basement from love".)

"Paid professionals" is a common trope used whenever there are large, or particularly effective, groups of people voicing their discontent in public. If it is conservatives questioning the legitimacy of liberal protests, this is often accompanied with the vaguely, or sometimes explicitly, anti-Semitic invocation of the name George Soros, a wealthy donor to many progressive causes, a Jewish man, and the supposed marionette artist behind progressive movements.

The goal of that labeling is to discredit the protesters by attacking their motives and their integrity. If they are benefiting financially from participating in the protest, then their concerns should not be taken seriously, because they don't really mean it. On a deeper level, this particular insult questions their character, insinuating that if they are the kind of people who, for financial gain, would publicly pretend to believe things they don't and thereby subvert democratic processes through subterfuge, then they are not people of character and should be ignored. Accusations of insincerity silence the message by impugning the messenger.

Often, that charge is spurious, but not always. Fake protests do occur, and they seem to be on the rise. Whereas grassroots campaigns arise from organizing among people who are concerned about a particular issue, artificially manufactured grassroots campaigns, which compensate people to espouse views that they do not necessarily hold, are known as "astroturf." As Sharyl Attkison wrote in her book *The Smear*:

> Astroturf is when political, corporate, or other special interests disguise themselves and try to represent their causes as being genuine groundswells of support by ordinary people.

"astroturf is when political, corporate, or other special interests disguise themselves and try to represent their causes as being genuine groundswells of support by ordinary people. Astroturfers write blogs, use social media, publish ads and letters to the editor, pay people to form protests or demonstrate as crowds, or simply post comments online to try to fool you into thinking an independent or grassroots movement is speaking."

According to Attkison, sports teams were among the first to establish fake Facebook accounts to "friend" their star athletes, in the guise of attractive women, so that the team management could get an anonymous view into their players' personal lives.

It is notoriously difficult to know how much social media posting is deceptive, in terms of people intentionally projecting the false impression of "groundswells of support by ordinary people," but it is certainly common. Dishonest paid "experts" are also sometimes classified as astroturfing, and such testimonials are worthy of our skepticism and research, but that begins to be outside our conversation on manufactured movements.

Entergy, an energy company based in New Orleans that serves customers in Arkansas, Louisiana, Mississippi, and Texas, paid a PR firm $55,000 to hire protestors to attend a City Council meeting and speak in favor of a new power plant they hoped to build. "Crowds On Demand," a Beverly Hills-based PR company, which brazenly claims that they provide their clients with "protests, rallies, flash-mobs, paparazzi events and other inventive PR stunts," did just that for Entergy. The City Council meeting was packed with dozens of people wearing identical t-shirts reading, "Clean Energy. Good Jobs. Reliable Power." The power plant was approved, 6-1.

As reported in New Orleans' *The Lens*, Keith Keough, one of the actors hired for that meeting, said that he and other fake protestors were paid "to sit through the meeting and clap every time someone said something against wind and solar power." Each hired attendee was paid $60, and those with speaking roles were paid $200.

When the astroturf story came out, there was an investigation, and Entergy was fined five million dollars, but in February of 2019, the City Council voted unanimously to let Entergy keep its permit to build the plant.

In truth, astroturf in-person protests, meaning the hiring of masses of people to publicly espouse views that are not their own, are rare, but as the Entergy example shows, they exist.

There is an important line to draw, though, between people who are literally hired to argue for beliefs that they do not hold, and people who are deeply committed to a cause and are financially supported in their work by others committed to that cause. Admittedly that line can be hard to draw, and we may be inclined to be more sympathetic to the side of an issue with which we agree. It is hard to hear the Entergy story and not be repulsed by that kind of overt corporate deception. But I celebrate that legitimate community organizers get paid to do the work they do. That is not at all the same thing.

I can't help but think again of PEG Partners, the non-profit organization that Deanna and I founded in 2004. For the first ten years, we had no paid staff, and I ran the organization as a volunteer. I was passionate about the work and had built relationships in the communities that PEG worked to support, but I also owned my own business as a musician and traveled nearly two hundred days a year—work about which I was also passionate. I also owed it to my wife and young son not to work every minute I was home. We were doing good work, but PEG had to fit into some pretty slim spaces in my life.

Over that first decade, it became clear that PEG could not grow and reach its potential with that model. In 2014, we hired a part-time executive director, and PEG expanded in beautiful directions because there was someone who could devote consistent time and attention to its operation. There is value in being paid for the work about which you are most passionate, partly because it allows you to give it more of your time and energy. Expecting all activists and organizers to be volunteers can be crippling to movements, and valuing the skills of gifted organizers is essential to keeping those skilled organizers from burning out or being faced with having to choose between being present for their families and acting on their other convictions.

> There is value in being paid for the work about which you are most passionate, partly because it allows you to give it more of your time and energy.

As Leo Gertner and Moshe Marvit wrote in the *Washington Post*, "Political and grassroots organizing and paid work are not inherently contradictory, as some would have us believe. [Not only can one] do deeply committed political work and be paid; it is often necessary for the long slog that campaigns require."

They go on to point out that Rosa Parks was attacked as a plant in her time. Parks was paid for her work with the NAACP and had received support from the Durr family, leading liberals in Montgomery who helped to raise money for her to attend the Highlander Folk School. Gertner and Marvit pose the compelling question, "[What] if we thought of Parks as a 'paid protester'? Would her protest be worth less?" The answer is no.

Things are not always what they seem to be at first glance. Astroturf is real, and powerful interests will sometimes make efforts to present a picture that is not accurate. That said, we should be cautious about claiming that campaigns are artificially manufactured just because we disagree with their goals. Most are not. As political comic John Oliver argues, "[The] danger of astroturfing may well be outweighed by the danger of believing that it is everywhere." He goes on to say, "While skepticism is healthy, cynicism—real cynicism—is toxic."

As I wrestle with what to do with these blurry lines, I can only hold on to that idea: skepticism is healthy, cynicism is toxic. It is a little too easy to question the motivations of others because motivations are usually mixed and almost impossible to prove.

Toxic Movements

Scott Shepherd grew up in a violent home in Indianola, Mississippi. He lived with an alcoholic father, and lacked adults in his life who boosted his self-confidence. Without many resources, he didn't excel in academics, or sports. He got beat up a lot.

In high school, Scott met some students who befriended him. They wanted him to hang out with them, and they told him that he had value after all, because he was White. They protected him. He was invited to meetings where people told him the problems he faced were mostly the fault of Black people, Jews, and immigrants. White people needed to stick together, they said.

> We should be cautious about claiming that campaigns are artificially manufactured just because we disagree with their goals. Most are not.

California State University professor Stanley S. Taylor writes in the International Journal of Sociology and Anthropology, "Inner conflicts and frustration can make a boy vulnerable to the lure of the gangs and their deviant behaviors. Gangs offer release from, and/or expression of, frustrations and bad feelings, protection from hostiles in the neighborhood, a peer group, and ways to make money, especially during the recruitment and socialization phases of gang membership." That was Scott's story, in a nutshell.

For the first time in his life, Scott had found a group of friends who had his back, and at the age of seventeen, he joined them in the Ku

Klux Klan. Over the following years, he rose through the ranks and became a Grand Dragon.

White Supremacy is a movement. It is not astroturfing but a group of people who are sincerely committed to a cause and are working toward what they believe is a better world, as toxic as that vision is. According to Scott, when he first heard people discussing the Klan in Indianola, they said it was a group that was "fighting for equal rights for White people." The organizers of the infamous Unite the Right rally in Charlottesville, Virginia, described themselves as a movement, and Austin Kessler, who pulled the parade permit for that event, cited Saul Alinsky as a valuable resource in his organizing education.

So, it's important to mention that movements are not noble simply by virtue of being movements. Some play on the politics of grievance to marginalize other people, to hold on to power that is unjustly denied to others, and to abuse them simply because of their identities.

> Movements are not noble simply by virtue of being movements.

The same dynamics of a movement apply, though. The movement gains power when it grows in numbers, when a lot of people do a little bit each. In this case, though, that growth is the outcome I want to prevent. We have seen the damage done by this kind of ideology, and the power of online chat groups where these hatreds can be stoked and supported. As I write today, news is continuing to emerge about an eighteen-year-old White man who killed ten people in a grocery store in Ohio because he believed and feared that people of color are taking over the country, or are "replacing" white people and white supremacy. The damage done by this rhetoric is real.

The Klan is no longer the dominant representation of White Supremacism in the United States. In the Southern Poverty Law Center's 2021 compilation of statistics on hate groups in the United States, the Klan only accounts for 18 of 733 hate groups they are tracking, a decline from 25 in 2020. The robes and hoods of the KKK have become visual shorthand for racism, but the organization itself, or more accurately, the loose band of organizations that constitute the Klan, is weak.

I wish this were due to a decline in overt racism in the United States, but it is not. A more mainstream version of White supremacist ideology has become dominant: clean-cut young White men in polo shirts rather than robes and hoods. It is important to note that the most damaging form of racism in our current society is not the overt racism that screams epithets but the quiet systemic racism that marginalizes people through denied opportunities, often carried out by people who would never consider themselves racist. Still, it is worth considering how people are recruited to active White supremacist movements, which have undoubtedly been growing in recent years.

There is a fundamental difference between justice movements (which are fundamentally rooted in love and the widening of our circles) and toxic movements (which are fundamentally rooted in fear and exclusion). It is tragically ironic that the acceptance, security, and belonging used as a recruitment tool in toxic movements comes at the expense of the exclusion, marginalization, and endangerment of others outside of the movement.

> If we hope to counter toxic movements, we need to move beyond expressing outrage or despair and think about what actually works.

As White supremacist ideology has grown and found outlets in social and mainstream media, it is clear that loudly condemning people is not a sufficient response. If we hope to counter toxic movements, we need to move beyond expressing outrage or despair and think about what actually works. Yelling at people and calling them stupid does not convince them to change, it strengthens their in-group bonds.

Plenty has been written on gang recruitment and intervention, and many of the lessons regarding how to help people exit those organizations apply to toxic movements. It is essential to develop real relationships, to acknowledge and affirm their agency in their own decisions, identify role models, and point out possibilities for other paths. To paraphrase popular author Stephen Covey, change moves at the speed of trust.

In a public setting, however, the rules and strategies must be different. If a Klan rally is happening in your town square, it won't be effective to go and listen, seek to form relationship, and ask compassionate but insightful questions. We have to interrupt and publicly subvert such public messages of hatred, or they will be allowed to stand.

Conversions rarely happen in that context, though. They are much more likely to happen as they did to Scott Shepherd.

Because of his Klan involvement, Scott was on the FBI's radar. After having dinner in a restaurant in Nashville one night, he was pulled over by the police, in what he described as an "ocean of blue lights." Scott had been drinking, and he failed the sobriety test. He also had an illegal, unregistered assault rifle in his truck. He was up against some jail time.

> Offering a wider circle, deeper support, acceptance, and forgiveness to those caught up in exclusionary ideologies seems to be the most fruitful approach.

When he tells the story, Scott says, "I came up with a plan [to] pull one of the oldest tricks in the book." He decided to check himself into a residential facility for alcohol and drug treatment, spend a month there, then go back to his life and use that certificate to convince the judge to reduce his sentence.

As it turned out, though, that experience was not a sham: it was transformative. Sobriety changed his perspective significantly. But a second transformation came from going through the program with two Black men to whom he became close and to whose stories he deeply related. It became too much for him to hold on to his racist views in the face of this evidence and these relationships. Quitting the Klan came at a significant cost; he received death threats, and his best friend was beaten severely and told to "talk to Scott."

It seems that human relationship is the key both to building movements and to tearing them down. Offering a wider circle, deeper support, acceptance, and forgiveness to those caught up in exclusionary ideologies seems to be the most fruitful approach. It is also hard, messy, and a long-term proposition, but it's what actually works, and it can be transformational for everyone involved, 'us' as well as 'them.'

In her popular TED talk, Megan Phelps-Roper, who grew up in the Westboro Baptist Church, tells the story of her exit from the cult. Discussing a man who established a relationship with her, originally through online arguments but eventually through genuinely curious conversation, she said, "We'd started to see each other as human beings, and it changed the way we spoke to one another." The humanization of people she had been condemning brought up cognitive dissonance that she eventually had to face. Their humanization of her, in spite of the hateful rhetoric in which she engaged, led to her transformation.

The acknowledgment that astroturfing and toxic movements add complexity to the landscape of social action could easily become yet another excuse for inaction. Yet it would be self-serving and cynical to exempt ourselves from the responsibilities that come with living in a democracy by concluding that all activism is a manufactured ruse. The best way to check the sincerity of a given effort may be to show up and get involved. I assure you that there are many people of integrity working hard for a better world. They are waiting for us to join them.

10

Community

"If you want to go fast, go alone. If you want to go far, go together."

—African proverb[13]

Until the most recent chapter of history, community was a given. As clown activist Patch Adams writes in his book *House Calls*:

> Throughout most of human history, a community was a tribe, and later a village. Initially, community offered protection, safety and insurance against any threats that came along. Today, in the absence of tribal communities, many people must be responsible for their own security. I think that our society's high level of anxiety is mainly due to this loss of belonging.

In the era, country, and neighborhood in which I live, community no longer happens automatically. We have to seek it out and create it if we find it to be of value. It is entirely possible to live one's life with very little in-person contact with the people in the closest geographic proximity and very little awareness of what binds us together in relationship.

This isn't how it has to be, and it's not the case everywhere. In the places I have traveled, places that people in wealthy nations call

---

[13]"African proverb" can sound like a dubious and nebulous attribution, but I encountered these words not only on a poster on the wall of a Zambian pastor's office, but also written in large letters on the wall of the Johannesburg airport in South Africa, so it seems accurate in this case.

"developing countries"—India, Guatemala, Haiti, Zambia, and others—the value of community has remained far more culturally intact. In rural villages in particular, people know each other, and are intimately aware of their neighbors' struggles and celebrations. They live in the context of deep community. They would think it bizarre not to.

The social isolation that is increasingly prevalent in my own context is also not the norm in all regions and communities in the United States. More private lifestyles are much less common in under-resourced neighborhoods, for instance, where space is at a premium.

In my own middle-class White context, relationships with our own next-door neighbors are often reduced to a mere nodding acquaintance, if we know them at all. It is true that via technology we are much more connected to people far away from us than we used to be, but those distant relationships often seem more disposable and temporary. It is as easy to unplug from them as it is to plug in. As sociologist John Brueggemann writes in his book *Rich, Free, and Miserable*, "There is a correlation between physical proximity and the 'moral intensity' people feel about a given situation. We tend to be more conscientious when we pay attention to the problems nearby."

This is a significant problem for people living in this more isolated social context, especially if we believe in the Movement Narrative of change, but it's not an unsolvable one. We have the capacity to create and develop community if we value it. If we want to work for positive change, this should be one of our top priorities.

Neighbors

I lived in the same small house on a busy road in my small town for about twenty-five years. I bought it in my twenties, and spent years fixing it up, and I know what the inside of every wall in that house looks like. The house is on a corner, and the corner only recently got a stop sign. Four of them, actually.

Before the stop signs, the traffic came through fast, and often loud. I loved that little house, and found it a peaceful place, but mufflers aren't really in vogue around there.

Perhaps an even bigger change than the stop signs happened years before, when the town invested in sidewalks. Before that, it was a death-defying proposition to walk down that road. There was one couple who did it often, and the gentleman in that couple was blind. I feared for their safety every time I saw them, and I was very happy the day the dedication ceremony took place for the new sidewalk, though I was amused that very few people walked to it. It took us a little while to get used to this new option.

Over time, though, the sidewalk had a transformative effect on the neighborhood. Because people were walking to the park, walking their dogs, and pushing baby strollers, people began to know each other, and to weave a web of connection. Exposure led to recognition, and small talk sometimes led to relationship. Those thin strands of connection sometimes deepened, but even the thin strands were of value when something more difficult came up and those neighbors had to work through it.

Before the sidewalk, it was hard to know the people beyond our immediate neighbors. Afterward, it became a bit more of a community. And in a town without a great deal of diversity, we had quite a lot of diversity there. Within three houses in each direction, we had diversity of race, gender, age, politics, religion, ability, sexual orientation, income, and more; and for the most part, it worked pretty well.

> Then the election of 2016 happened, and I felt as if the town had ripped the sidewalks out.

Then the election of 2016 happened, and I felt as if the town had ripped the sidewalks out. People weren't talking with each other, for fear that things might get ugly. Some were terrified and despairing, some were happy and hopeful, and if we found that we were on opposite sides of that divide, it was hard to know how to relate.

Decisions we make to choose leaders at the highest level of government are not like football team allegiances. People live and die by those decisions. Lives are saved and ruined by them. This mattered, and it was not unreasonable to be emotionally invested. I was among those with very strong feelings about this, and I still am.

That said, I was heartbroken to watch the fabric of my community torn in two.

One night not long after the election, I was talking with my wife and son, then seven, at the dinner table, and speaking my frustration. "I just want to hang a sign on the house," I said, "that says 'If your car battery is dead, you can knock on my door. No matter who you voted for, I will give you a jump.'"

Then it occurred to me that I *did* know how to have signs made, so we started to talk about what such a sign should say. We eventually came up with the text here, and I had a canvas banner made for the house—over eight feet tall.

I should say that, at first, Mason was concerned about it. He thought it might make people angry, and it's true that we slept in the bedroom right behind the wall where it was hanging, so if anyone had taken a shot at the sign, we could have been harmed. I explained to him that it really was a sign of welcome, though, and that I didn't think there was a significant danger. I also explained that there are some things I need to stand up for even if it is dangerous, and this felt like one of them.

He was convinced, and on Christmas Eve of 2016, he helped me nail the sign to the front of our house. It reads: "You are our neighbors. No matter who you vote for, your skin color, where you are from, your faith, or who you love, we will try to be here for you. That's what community means. Let's be neighbors." This was very much on the front end of the trend of people putting statements of belief in their yards, and it differs significantly from many of them, in that it invites relationship across one of our most difficult boundaries—politics.

In the weeks, months, and years following, I had lots of conversations with people on that sacred sidewalk, people who'd been inspired by the sign.

YOU are our neighbors. No matter who you vote for, your skin color, where you are from, your faith, or who you love, we will try to be here for you. That's what community means. Let's be neighbors.

©2016   letsbeneighbors.org

The Let's Be Neighbors banner.

One person told me they had actually moved to the neighborhood because they saw it there. Most reactions were positive. The only real pushback I got was about the political piece. A couple of friends said, "I just can't go with the 'No matter who you vote for...' part."

I would agree with them, if the sentence ended differently. It doesn't say, "everything's cool," or "let's be nice." It says "we will try to be here for you."

I am deeply convinced that real transformation happens in the context of relationship. People are seldom rejected into making more compassionate decisions. When we know each other, we have the capacity to see things in new light, and to humanize rather than dehumanize. That, in itself, is a victory, because in dehumanizing others, we lose a bit of our own humanity. In re-humanizing, we gain some of it back, even if no one switches sides.

As naïve and saccharine as it may sound, the empirical truth that I've observed is that people are healed by love. Practical, generous, accountable love expressed in tangible action. If the only goals are to defeat and humiliate the opposition, then where does that lead?

> In dehumanizing others, we lose a bit of our own humanity. In re-humanizing, we gain some of it back, even if no one switches sides.

Peacemaking doesn't mean coming to a point where everyone agrees. We will never reach that point, nor should we. Peacemaking means, in part, that we find our way together while disagreeing, and together, hammer out systems that protect the marginalized and treat people fairly. This re-weaving of the fabric of society requires a generosity of spirit that can be hard to summon, but is possible.

In a dramatic historical example, I think of dissident activist and longtime political prisoner Nelson Mandela inviting his prison guard to his inauguration as the president of South Africa. There was a vision there for a profoundly unusual way of responding to the dehumanization he had endured. He chose to humanize his oppressor and treat him with respect, modeling the path to healing.

That's not to say that knowing each other always leads to warm relationship. It does not. But not knowing each other makes it extremely easy to demonize and dehumanize people with whom we disagree. Limiting contact is a key ingredient for bigotry, and deepening relationship generally leads to re-humanization.

People began to ask where they can get a sign like the one on my house, so I created a Web site where anyone could download the art for free (or for whatever they wanted to pay) and print their own. I hired a Web designer to create the site and a graphic designer to lay out several versions of it, including a yard sign version, and a Spanish version. Some people wrote and asked me to have them printed for them, so I eventually added that option as well, so now people can buy a sign through the Web site if they would like to, but the free option is still there.

> Peacemaking doesn't mean coming to a point where everyone agrees. We will never reach that point, nor should we.

Gradually, people have hung these signs on homes, businesses, and churches across the country, including a large one on Abraham Lincoln's church in Springfield, Illinois. People write and share stories on the Web site of conversations and reactions they have experienced.[14] Clearly, strands of community have been woven because of it.

Community has no place in the Hero Narrative, which is one more indication that this narrative is neither helpful nor true. If we want to have a positive impact in the world, community is essential. So where is yours?

If that question is not easy to answer, perhaps it is better to ask, "How will you find or create it?"

Showing Up

In 2011, on the tenth anniversary of the September 11 attacks, I found myself fighting downtown New York City traffic. I had been invited to lead a remembrance service that morning at a Presbyterian church

---

[14]Download the art, read stories, etc. at letsbeneighbors.org

in Woodbury, New Jersey. It was a difficult but meaningful service; I tried to hold in the same hand the pain and loss that people in that community had suffered—some quite directly—and also questions about how we had responded as a nation in the years since those attacks, and who we wish to become now.

When the service ended, I left all my gear set up, threw one of my guitars into the back of my car, and raced up to New York City for my next show, a concert called "Love Wins" honoring first responders and trying to make space for healing. New York City had not invited first responders to the official commemoration events of the day, and this event was created as an effort to honor their courage and sacrifices, as well as to offer a more restorative vision of how to move forward.

Though I was feeling the weight of the day's remembrance, I was also admittedly excited. I was on my way to perform with Pete Seeger, David Amram, Spook Handy, and other musicians I greatly admire. I could hardly imagine any better place to mark that day, or a better crowd of people with whom to do so.

In the months following the 9/11 attacks, my friend Lyndon Harris had headed up the relief efforts based at St. Paul's Chapel, which stands less than a hundred yards from the World Trade Center site but survived that day's attacks strangely unscathed. As a result, he became something of a national celebrity. With Lyndon's leadership, volunteers turned the sanctuary into a relief center, addressing the physical and emotional needs of the first responders and others working at the site. They provided food, massage, music, counseling, and space for naps on the pews; and they made a huge community effort to provide for countless other needs: material, emotional, and spiritual.

Lyndon showed up for his part in the crisis, but after that acute need had subsided and the church had returned to its more traditional role in the community, he turned his attention to the ongoing work of healing and forgiveness, not just from this specific instance of mass violence, but from violence all over the world. He established Gardens of Forgiveness, a non-profit organization which works to teach the skills and value of forgiveness and establishes places of refuge for people to contemplate forgiveness as it relates to their own experiences of trauma. There are now Gardens of Forgiveness in Long

Island, New York; Charleston, South Carolina; and Beirut, Lebanon, though the incredibly complicated political context of the World Trade Center site has thus far prevented the original goal of establishing a Garden of Forgiveness there.

On that day, as I tried to weave my way through the streets of Soho, people were busily setting up the room for the concert a few stories above me. Racing to fit both events into the same day, I arrived only after the concert had begun, though fortunately well before my slot in the program.

One of the stories that sticks with me from that day is one I was told by my longtime friend Sarah Hipp, who had helped to organize the concert. She told me that while setting up for the concert, the late and legendary folk singer Pete Seeger came in, looked at the room, and shook his head. The chairs, which were of the movable cushioned variety, were set in straight rows, forming a large rectangle with an aisle down the middle. As a seasoned organizer, Pete understood that there is nothing straight or rigid about community. If you want to create community, you have to welcome people into it; he wanted the chairs to curve.

> At ninety-two years old, Pete began moving each of the hundreds of chairs, one by one, until they served the community better.

Pete wasn't the kind of musician who expected people to serve as spectators to something he did for them. He wanted them to participate, both in singing the songs and in changing the world. He wanted to create real relationships and alliances and get people involved, not only with him but with each other. For that to happen at this concert, people needed to be able to see each other, to curl around each other physically as well as emotionally.

Pete Seeger was a legend, but he was no prima donna. He didn't issue orders or make demands. He didn't ask anyone to change the chairs, or even to help him move the chairs. He just started moving them.

At ninety-two years old, Pete began moving each of the hundreds of chairs, one by one, until they served the community better. He knew well that Gandhi did not say, "Demand the change you wish to see in the world." He said, "*Be* the change you wish to see in the world." Pete perceived a change that he wished to see, so he got to work. He did the same thing with litter, picking it up everywhere he went.

When Sarah expressed some concern for him doing the manual labor of moving those chairs, he responded by saying, "Oh, it's OK. I didn't get to chop wood today." He was not one to sit idly by when there was work to do, and he led by example.

Showing up means more than being physically present in a situation; it means participating where you show up, in whatever big or small way that place and that moment demand.

It's not surprising that others in the room noticed what Pete was doing, and he soon found himself accompanied by more people moving chairs. The job was done quickly, and the event was better for it. Pete Seeger was in the business of making space for community, and he did so not by haranguing or cajoling others. He simply began, and people noticed. And because the work he did was so inspiring, people joined in. They wanted to be a part of it, and they wanted to hear more of the story. In the process, they found each other.

Showing up and getting to work is how things get done. It's another narrative that we sometimes get backwards. We think that people

with Pete Seeger in New York on Sept. 11, 2011

who have a big impact start out with a great plan, recruit the support team they need, and then implement it. In fact, most of them start out by showing up, beginning, and recruiting and revising as they go.

My brother-in-law Eric, who lives just up the road from me in Asheville, has spent a lot of his life following his nose into things that interest him. He's a computer guy who also has a deep sense of the importance of civic engagement. Following those passions, he started connecting with some people in the community who also care about things he cares about in a group called Code for Asheville. Together they started meeting with some city government officials, and one of the things he realized as he learned more about the city was that it is extremely difficult for most people to figure out what the city government is actually doing. So Eric and some other volunteers created a Web site that makes the city budget easy to see, using graphic interfaces and telescoping levels of detail. It gives average citizens a way to be more engaged with their local government, and it increases transparency, which is good for the whole community. Now he has done the same for other municipalities.

That work led to Eric taking a job working for the city, where he is engineering positive change and transparency from the inside.

Of course, when we take action, we open ourselves to criticism. Showing up and getting to work is an inherently vulnerable thing to do, whether it takes the form of speaking up in a conversation, going to a workshop, writing a letter to a newspaper, or visiting (or joining) the folks camping out in the park to protest an injustice. It's how our most meaningful work generally begins, though. We have to decide to show up.

Unexpected Connection

Several years ago, I went to Big Spring, Texas, at the invitation of a Presbyterian church in the area, to spend a few days leading workshops and having conversations. This is west Texas, spacious, flat, and dusty country, and my friend Matt Miles was the pastor there. Matt is also an EMT and a fireman; he's a full-on cowboy, complete with boots, tight jeans, pickup truck, and chewing tobacco. He is also well-versed in that particular brand of sardonic Texas wit that is sharper than a cactus spine.

One of the things we did with that time was hold a workshop on peacemaking. That probably doesn't sound too radical or edgy in most contexts, but this workshop took place in the early days of the Iraq War, when any concern expressed about whether the war was a good idea was often met with angry and serious accusations of treason. These were also the early years after the 9/11 attacks, and the whole nation seemed to be injured, angry, and prone to lashing out.

Add to that the facts that we were gathering thirty-nine miles up the road from Midland, where George W. Bush spent the early part of his childhood, and that he was the president at the time. Big Spring is the former home of Webb Air Force Base and the former headquarters of Cosden Oil. A big refinery remains, but Cosden and Webb are long gone, and both losses have been extremely costly for the town. This was not a town you would imagine as being particularly sympathetic to the peace movement.

We had a good conversation, though it was painful in places. There were military veterans there, as well as people with family currently serving in the military. There were plenty present who felt strongly that the Iraq War was necessary and right, and a very few who questioned it, which made the conversation heated on occasion.

These people were all trying to do the right thing, though they had wildly divergent perspectives on how to go about it. As we continued to talk, however, people became more comfortable. The conversation wasn't easy, but it was real, and the mood gently shifted as people began to believe it to be a safe space in which to be honest.

Well into our time together, one woman expressed some real reservations about the Iraq War; and later, another did too. The conversation went on for some time after that; I presented some ideas, but mostly, in that setting, my job was to create space for the conversation and to ask some constructive questions.

As we closed out the session, I recall one of those women saying that she was glad to have discovered that another woman there felt the way she did. Before that, she said, she felt she was the only one. These two women knew each other, but they had never known that they shared this view, presumably because they had been afraid to speak it or found no safe space in which to do so. The two of them found each other, and presumably some comfort and inspiration, because they showed up *for* the conversation that day, and then they showed up *in* the conversation.

This is another argument for showing up, both literally and metaphorically: it's really the only way we can find each other. It's the only way to create healthy community with a sense of connectedness. And community, as costly and messy as it is, is our best way forward.

What Makes A Community?

Of course, the word *community* is another nebulous bit of vocabulary. People have often used the word to refer to our physical neighborhoods or towns. In recent years we have re-defined it to include communities of cause, communities of classification (for instance, "the LGBTQ+ community" or "the Asian and Pacific Islander community"), and virtual communities of people who share common interests or goals, though they may have never met in person. In all of these contexts, the word community indicates interrelatedness—relationships that are woven between multiple people that provide the context for our connection and our actions together.

> Community, as costly and messy as it is, is our best way forward.

My friend Hugh Hollowell founded an organization in Raleigh, North Carolina, called Love Wins. Love Wins is a community that serves, and is partly made up of, people who are experiencing homelessness. He argues that homelessness is not fundamentally an economic problem but rather a problem of community. If my house burned down tonight, I would not be homeless because there are people in my community, both family and friends, who would take me in. Many people whom we call homeless are without shelter primarily because they have run out of people to call.

In general, I have been writing in this book about communities of cause—people who are working toward similar goals together. It is important to acknowledge, though, that there will never be a community of human beings who will be completely aligned in their thoughts, values, and approaches. Conflict within communities, though more evident in some than others, is always a part of what it means to work together, and it is often a good thing.

Communities that are not chosen based on agreement, but rather exist through circumstance, such as our neighborhoods or towns—or even our families—are perhaps the most important places for us to work for positive change and our deepest sources of nourishment and growth when we can create healthy relationships and patterns, though often our hardest work. When we don't start from an assumption of common interests, we must work to find them. We will inevitably find that we have at least some common interests, and the process of discovering them can be enriching.

One of the fundamental principles of effective conflict mediation is the need to shift from *positions* to *interests*. As Roger Fisher and William Ury write in their small and seminal book *Getting To Yes*, "Behind opposed positions lie shared and compatible interests, as well as conflicting ones." For instance, siblings may disagree about how best to care for their aging parents (positions), but they may deeply share a concern for their parents' welfare (interests).

> One of the fundamental principles of effective conflict mediation is the need to shift from positions to interests.

In the peace workshop in Big Spring, Texas, we found that after some solid conversation, people were eventually able to hear each other's concerns, fears, and perspectives more respectfully, even if they still disagreed passionately about the best course to take. Most of the people in the room supported the war in Iraq. A few opposed it. But everyone in the room wanted their families to be safe. Some people in the room had supported their families through income derived from the military and had grown up in a military culture. They had a natural allegiance to the military's orientation and approaches to problems. They may also have held some understandable defensiveness to what they perceived as attacks on the integrity of military leaders whom they admired, including the Commander in Chief. Many of us in the room felt wounded and scared; some wanted retribution, believing that it might provide some comfort or that it was what was right.

Others may have had experiences of violence and retribution in their own lives that led them to question whether violence can ever be a path toward growth and healing. Some may have perceived this latest iteration of organized violence (war) as part of an ongoing pattern that needed to be stemmed rather than replicated.

Everybody, though, wanted to feel safe, and for some time after the September 11 attacks, very few people in the United States did. I have written a fair amount in this book about the need to humanize our heroes rather than seeing them as "other," but it is at least as important, if not more so, that we humanize our opponents. That is sometimes an extremely challenging task, especially as we have the increasing opportunity to "silo" ourselves into social contexts where we mostly encounter only people who think more or less like we do.

> Everybody, though, wanted to feel safe, and for some time after the September 11 attacks, very few people in the United States did.

When we can manage to stop and listen to each other's perspectives, I have frequently seen a shift occur in contentious conversations. We may not convince each other, but by listening to them, we are less dismissive of people with whom we disagree because we understand the interests beneath their positions. If we can articulate, acknowledge, and agree on the commonality of some of those interests, we have a productive starting place to move toward meeting them.

In the example from Texas, there were people there who felt unsafe and believed that war in Iraq would make us safer (by eliminating a threat and an enemy and by increasing regional stability through military might). There were also people there who felt unsafe and believed that war in Iraq would make us even less safe (by diverting resources needed elsewhere and generating animosity toward the U.S. that would create more enemies where they didn't exist before, haunting us for generations to come and further destabilizing the region). There were many other reasons people believed that the Iraq War was the right or wrong course of action, but those two make for a useful illustration, since they point to the same goal—being and feeling safe.

At that point, if we are really listening to each other, we have the opportunity to relate to each other across the lines of the conflict: "I get what you're saying. You love your kids, and you want them to be OK. We disagree on how best to achieve that, but I get it."

In doing so, we restore some of each other's humanity and some of our own, whether or not we come to agreement on how best to move forward. Ironically, a small shift like that can make the world feel a bit safer and actually *be* a bit safer; and that, after all, was the goal in the first place.

Harmony Is Not Homogeneity

Communities of context, rather than of cause, are important. They give us the opportunity to do the crucial work of humanizing people who are different from us in various ways and who may see things differently than we do. The same is true, of course, in communities of cause, where we are among people with whom we largely agree. Seeing the mistakes we make together, adjusting our own perspectives as we learn from each other, and watching others adjust theirs—these small shifts help to subvert the Hero Narrative and thereby encourage our own action. Understanding our heroes' humanity can be extremely empowering.

Another deep value of work in community is coming to understand the practical value of diversity. When I begin workshops, I often begin with a "Diversity Welcome," which acknowledges the various kinds of diversity present in the room. It's a tool I learned at a "Trainer Training" put on by Training for Change in Detroit years ago, and have modified over the years. I welcome people who are feeling energized, then people who are feeling weary. Then people who consider themselves leaders. Then people who do not consider themselves to be leaders. People who are gay. People who are straight. People who don't feel as if either of those terms applies to them. Then people of faith. Then people who claim no faith. People who feel at home in this group, who are "from here," or who are deeply involved with the topic. People who are uncomfortable in this group, who consider themselves outsiders, who are just beginning to explore this topic. I take a moment to welcome the women in the room. I take a moment to welcome the men. I welcome people who don't feel as if either of those terms is big enough to hold all of who they are. People with skin the color of walnut, cedar, pine, or ebony. People who consider themselves young. People who no longer consider themselves young. I welcome Republicans and Democrats and people who support other parties, as well as people who support no party. Sometimes, I welcome people in each decade of age that is represented.

Depending on the situation, I change my way of doing the welcome a bit each time, but I almost always find it to have a powerful effect. I look people in the eye and take my time with it because I really mean it. Diversity is not just a matter of political correctness. Having different identities, perspectives, and life experiences in the room enriches a gathering, especially when the gathering is for the purpose of discerning a way forward together. And the word 'welcome' doesn't really cover it, given that most of us have had the experience of hearing that word spoken in spaces where we felt distinctly unwelcome.

> As with music, notes sung or played in unison are simply not as rich as the combination of many different notes singing or playing in harmony.

Diversity of perspective and experience can lend depth, richness, and subtlety to our work in the same way that musical notes in harmony can lend depth, richness, and subtlety to music, so it is an important goal and value not just because it pushes back against marginalization, but because our work will be better work because it includes more perspectives.

Harmony has always been a fascinating word to me, since it bridges my lifelong interests in music and peace work. As a synonym for *peace*, however, I think that harmony is often misunderstood. It cannot, by definition, mean homogeneity. That's unity, not harmony. And just as with music, notes sung or played in unison are simply not as rich as the combination of many different notes singing or playing in harmony. We need diversity for that.

Of course, it is also true that many notes playing together may clearly *not* be in harmony with one another. Creating that confluence takes intention, patience, and work. It is a beautiful thing when we achieve it, though. And it is not achieved by eliminating difference, but instead by finding ways to work together that are mutually nourishing, that honor and reveal each other's gifts, that tune those differences into harmony with each other.

We have better ideas in community, too, though many of us resist that idea.

In their insightful book *Switch: How to Change Things When Change Is Hard*, Chip and Dan Heath cite a fascinating study in which a group of people was asked to generate and consider possible solutions for a parking problem on a college campus. They were first asked to list all of the solutions they could think of on their own; then a panel of experts assessed the ideas to determine which were the best. In the end, they came up with a short list of recommendations, based on the many suggestions that had been made.

> We have a demonstrable tendency to overestimate our own capacity to solve problems in the absence of others' input.

The interesting part came when they were asked afterward how many of the good ideas they had come up with personally and how many had been generated by others in the group. Consistently, people overestimated how many of the "good" ideas they had thought of on their own. On average, they each believed that they had come up with 75 percent of the best ideas, when in reality, they had come up with 30 percent of them. It turns out that we have a demonstrable tendency to overestimate our own capacity to solve problems in the absence of others' input.

Maybe that's not too surprising. By definition, we each see the world from our own perspective, so what seems "right" to us is what our own experience has confirmed. Most of us think we have a pretty good handle on how the world works, so it seems somewhat natural that we tend to undervalue others' perspectives when they differ from our own or bring experience that we have not had. But while it may be natural to stick with our own ideas, it is demonstrably less effective in addressing problems and working for positive change.

Who Is At The Table?

Another significant value of working in community is that if we are truly engaged with our communities, then more stakeholders are represented in the conversation. If we want to work on issues of homelessness and don't welcome into the conversation the people most directly affected—people who are without housing—then we are unlikely to meet our goals. That seems like an obvious error, but it is a common one. If we have those conversations among people who are experiencing homelessness and people who are concerned about their needs, but we fail to include in that conversation social workers, local businesses, law enforcement, people already working on the issue, etc., then we are also unlikely to come up with the best strategies to meet everyone's needs, and the solutions we propose are unlikely to be sustainable.

This is particularly true among groups that locate themselves more in the mainstream than in the margins. It is fundamental to the nature of privilege that it is harder to see what's happening when one is in the middle; it's easier from the margins. Being privileged doesn't mean that someone is bad or good; it simply means that there are things they don't have to think about that others do. Because both of my legs work well to transport me without assistance, I don't always think much about whether it is necessary to go up a few stairs to enter a building. Some folks I care about have to consider that barrier carefully. If I want to understand the issue and how best to deal with it, it is essential that I listen to friends who have mobility issues.

This means that White people, men, cisgender people, heterosexuals, people with no obvious physical or mental disabilities, wealthy people, people in mainstream religious groups, etc. must be extremely intentional about listening and learning. That is important as a means, because it builds understanding, but also in order to achieve effective ends. Power tends to be concentrated among people who are privileged and among people who are accustomed to having such power. It just seems "normal." If many of the voices in a community are not being heard, however, then the conclusions reached by the powerful will not be tenable for people outside of the mainstream. There is significant perspective and insight lacking, and the interests of all stakeholders are not being considered.

Once again, this work of community involves a heavy dose of listening. Listening skills, though manifestly teachable, are seldom taught, and that is to our detriment. Rather than telling each other what we think and asking others what they think, we tend to tell our opponents what *they* think. "Sure, but when you people say *this*, what you mean is *that*!" So we end up arguing with imaginary adversaries rather than hearing the concerns of real people, which tend to be a bit more nuanced than we imagine. That approach has not served us well, and it doesn't show much sign of serving us better in the future.

I've been taking this to heart lately in my own work and experimenting with bringing more voices into my own decision making, both in the creative areas of my life and in the business aspects. It has proven to have all the value that I had hoped. I enjoyed and benefited deeply from working with the editors of this book. They brought perspective that I don't have. I have enjoyed some great artistic collaborations on some songwriting I've done in recent years, as well. But the deepest ongoing effect that this new, community-centered approach has had for me is in the change I've made in the way I handle event bookings.

I have a tendency to say yes to too many invitations to speak and perform, and this has a very real cost for me, for my family, and eventually for the quality of my work. In an effort to do a better job with discernment and on the advice of some wise mentors, I have begun a new process in my own scheduling. I used to decide more or less on my own which engagement invitations I would accept, in consultation with my booking agent. Now, all booking decisions go through a booking committee.

That committee consists of my booking agent, my wife, and myself. We look at each invitation in the context of other calendar commitments around it as well as the various things I value in an invitation, which include not only the fee, but also the opportunity for impact, the chance that an event will lead to other good events, personal relationships, support for a cause in which I believe, and many other factors. Together, we do a much better job of considering those categories and their relative weight than I do by myself. As a result, I'm saner, less exhausted, and doing better work.

It's also appropriate that more stakeholders be represented. My calendar of commitments has significant effects on everyone at the meeting, especially my wife, Deanna. If she is involved in those decisions on the front end of the process, then we can make those choices together. Deanna has always been extraordinarily supportive of my work, although my frequent absences have real costs for her. With this new process, though, I think we are diminishing the likelihood of understandable resentments. We are making these decisions together.

Another advantage of working in community is that over time it brings an inherent accountability. By working together, we come to know and understand each other's strengths and weaknesses, our character and style; that elevates the quality of our work and also of our daily lives. People who show themselves to be dependable and invested tend to be highly valued in a community. People who are difficult and destructive are not. In my small town, for example, I have noticed that businesses that are run by disagreeable people tend not to last too long. Accountability is a part of the inherent beauty of community.

> Another advantage of working in community is that over time it brings an inherent accountability.

Not Alone

The last lens through which I examine community is *solidarity*. The term has become politically loaded, but it should not be dismissed by anyone who wants to have a positive impact, regardless of where they sit on the political spectrum. It's a term with evolving meanings, and I believe that I understand it now much better than I used to, after having spent my first night in jail.

I was arrested, along with six other men, in May of 2011 for disrupting the North Carolina Legislature from the balcony while the legislators below deliberated the largest cut to public education funding in the history of the state, changes to voter laws that would have the effect of suppressing minority votes, and the gutting of the North Carolina Racial Justice Act. This groundbreaking law allowed death penalty defendants to present evidence of racism in their cases as part of their defense and appeals process. If their claims were determined to have merit, their sentences could be reduced from death to life in prison. It did not set anyone free; it just allowed for appeals based on clear evidence of racism in their conviction or sentencing, and it prevented the state from killing someone if they won that appeal. It seems like common sense that death penalty defendants would be able to appeal if they have clear evidence of racism in their legal proceedings, but common sense is often lacking in the law.

The law had passed only two years before, and it was already under attack. The group with whom I was protesting was focusing on several issues, and I felt strongly about each of them. But it was the Racial Justice Act that went right to my core and convinced me to join them in a protest which might result in spending time in jail. Rev. Dr. William Barber, the head of the North Carolina NAACP, was the leader of the effort to challenge the goals of the current legislative majority. This action was an early iteration of what later turned into the Forward Together movement that has gained national and even international attention in the years since, due to their large and sustained Moral Monday protests.

That day, Rev. Barber and I stood with many others in the balcony overlooking the North Carolina House of Representatives while they were in session. Rev. Barber asked the Speaker of the House the same question that the prophet Micah had asked in the Bible, "What does the Lord require of you?"

Nearby protestors began chanting Micah's response to his own question, "Do justice. Love mercy. Walk humbly with God."

Seven people in the group were removed from the chamber, handcuffed, and taken in the backs of police cruisers to the jail, where we were charged with second degree trespassing and disorderly conduct. We were photographed, processed, fingerprinted, and taken to a holding cell, where we spent a few hours, with other prisoners occasionally coming and going. Each hour, on the hour, we took turns leading a prayer. We talked with the other people there about their situations. We sang, we told stories, and we talked strategy, deciding together that we would not post bail yet, though it was available to us. The intention of nonviolent resistance is to expose systemic injustice. If good and principled people are in jail, the reasoning goes, then perhaps there is some lack of goodness and principle in the system that is putting them there. We wanted to shine a little more light on the immorality of what was happening in the legislature, so we decided not to leave jail quite yet. Four of the group were pastors, and all of us were generally well-respected in our own communities.

While getting arrested for the first time was personally significant for me, I was quickly reminded of how small my place in the struggle for justice really was as I listened to dramatic stories told by Rev. Barber and Rev. Kojo Nantambu, who was around when the Wilmington Ten were arrested. As we sat together in the holding cell, Rev. Nantambu talked about the siege of the church where the African American community had gathered for refuge, how a man with whom he was standing arm in arm was shot and fell to the ground right beside him. Though these stories were hard to hear, they certainly put our current action into perspective, and it was a gift to me to hear them in that time and place. They shrank our own situation and sacrifice down to size.

> If good and principled people are in jail, the reasoning goes, then perhaps there is some lack of goodness and principle in the system that is putting them there.

Nevertheless, I was scared. I didn't know what was going to happen, and I had little to no control over the situation. Even as I understood that this action was quite small in the history of the struggle for civil rights, it was a big deal for me personally.

When we were admitted, we were taken out of the room one at a time. I was stripped of all of my clothing, the contents of my pockets, and my wedding ring (one of the few times it has left my finger since I first put it on). I was searched, standing naked before a prison guard who made me spread my feet apart and adjust my body so that he had a good view. I was given orange-striped prison clothes, several sizes too large.

After we had each been through that same routine and waited a while longer, we were manacled by one wrist to a chain connecting eight prisoners and led through an elevator to the general holding cells. It had been several hours by this time, but the lights were still on, and the prisoners were still sitting at tables playing games or standing around in the common area when we arrived. We were each told to grab a thin, plastic-covered mattress from a stack outside the door and then go inside.

Just inside the door, facing us, was a muscular man with dreadlocks and tattoos covering his neck and all the visible parts of his arms and chest. He grinned and said, "Welcome to Cell Block Green, gentlemen." Though I tried to figure it out, I had no idea whether that smile and welcome were friendly or not. I decided to assume that they were. The remote-controlled steel and glass door moved into place behind us, the sound of its whirring motor ending in a metallic locking sound.

The jail was overcrowded, and the cells were all full, so some of us slept (or rather, lay down) on the floor in the common area along with roughly two dozen other prisoners. I felt vulnerable, so sleep was out of the question for me.

I cannot imagine going through the arrest and night in jail without those other men with me. The powerful solidarity of that experience will stay with me forever. I will not forget Rev. Nantambu smiling and leading our manacled prisoner train in a tight U-turn in the jail's elevator (no buttons on the inside, just a camera) so we would be pointing the right way when the door opened again. Or Rev. Barber leading songs and prayers, educating us, and keeping spirits up. The dignity and grace of Rev. Spearman and the others. The joking

> It's the deepest gift of such a struggle— knowing in your bones that you are not alone.

and processing of what was going on. That's how we get through the hardest days and the hardest work we face. As my friend Chuck Brodsky sings, "We keep each other going and we show each other signs." It's the deepest gift of such a struggle—knowing in your bones that you are not alone.

It may seem contradictory to include this story about spending a night in jail when I've just spent so many pages arguing for the importance and effectiveness of small efforts. Depending on your life experience, jail may or may not seem like a very big deal, but it likely sounds rather drastic

Rev. Kojo Nantambu, Rev. Curtis Gatewood, and myself

when compared to some of the efforts I've described so far—making copies or going to meetings, for example. Regardless, I don't think it undermines the argument for small efforts.

More dramatic and seemingly larger efforts and sacrifices are sometimes necessary, and they are sometimes yours to do. But they are not the sensible starting place. It is not wise to walk into the gym and try to pick up the heaviest weights you see. You have to work out and increase your strength and stamina, and learn good technique. For that, you need mentors and teachers, who are most easily found in community. The first step, though, and arguably the hardest one, is actually showing up at the gym—or the meeting.

Community is a powerful force for change. In our arrest at the State House, no one of us alone would have caused the media attention or community discussion that we all did together: five Black, two White; four ministers, one musician. We generated a fair amount of conversation, and though the gutting of the North Carolina Racial Justice Act passed, it was vetoed by the governor and narrowly missed having enough votes for an override. I'd like to think we had something to do with one or both of those last points, just by getting people talking about the issue, perhaps serving as the catalyst for some of them to contact their representatives and encourage the governor to veto the bill.

> In community, in the context of real and interwoven relationships, we can support, nourish, educate, and challenge each other in ways that are constructive rather than destructive.

In the weeks that followed our arrests, I saw comment after comment on social media saying, "I had no idea that this was happening!" Now people did. That was our goal. We achieved it.

Most of us are understandably busy with our lives and other obligations, and it is no wonder that we fail to keep up with everything happening in our state capitols. It is our duty, in a democracy, to keep up with it, but it is not surprising that we often miss the mark. Those comments were what I wanted to see—that people who didn't know before did now.

In community, in the context of real and interwoven relationships, we can support, nourish, educate, and challenge each other in ways that are constructive rather than destructive. We can devise more effective and wiser strategies in community than we can create on our own. We can hold each other accountable and catch each other when we stumble. We can move forward together, deep in the knowledge that we are not alone.

One last important thing about community: it's hard. Tuning our own notes together so that we are in harmony, while each one retains their own voice, is extremely difficult. Welcoming diversity of opinion and listening closely and compassionately while disagreeing is hard work. Finding ways to collaborate with people we find challenging is tough. Discerning where the lines are regarding when someone can no longer be welcomed into the community is hard. Showing up in situations where you have traditionally been disregarded is hard. Setting aside privilege and yielding power is hard.

According to my aforementioned friend Hugh Hollowell, there is only one thing that is harder: lack of community.

11

Creativity

If you have built castles in the air, your work need not be lost; that is where they should be. Now put the foundations under them.

—Henry David Thoreau

On May 26, 2007, the Ku Klux Klan gathered for a rally in Knoxville, Tennessee. The defendants in a local murder case were African American, and some White supremacists from out of town drove there to protest. The general tone of their rally was unsurprisingly hateful. One man in camouflage held up a hand-drawn poster with a picture of a noose and the words "insert neck here" scrawled beside it, expressing his preference for a lynching over a trial.

Most people in Knoxville were not pleased to have the Klan come to town, but how should they respond?

The most natural responses to aggression are fight and flight. On the one hand, we are tempted to go down to the rally and give our opponents a piece of our minds. "We'll see how tough they are when we have a bigger crowd, and we shout them down!"

On the other, we often say, "Ignore them. They just want attention," which is more or less a form of retreat.

The problem with the first approach is that it adds "deeper darkness to a night already devoid of stars," as Dr. King wrote. Meeting hatred with hatred only increases the amount of hatred in the world. That may sound idealistic, but I am convinced that it is the heart of pragmatism. In this particular case, the Klan *does* thrive on anger and opposition. They love it, and adding our hatred to theirs is no more effective in opposing their message than trying to put out a grass fire by dousing it with gasoline.

The problem with the second approach, in its most usual form of 'just staying home,' is that it allows damaging and hateful rhetoric to be broadcast unopposed.[15] Such rallies will nearly always gather a crowd and media exposure, unless there is an organized effort to deny them one. When such hatred goes unopposed, the people who are being attacked by their rhetoric end up feeling abandoned by potential allies who could be standing with them.

> Adding our hatred to theirs is no more effective in opposing their message than trying to put out a grass fire by dousing it with gasoline.

They feel that way because they *are* being abandoned. "We will have to repent in this generation not merely for the hateful words and actions of the bad people but for the appalling silence of the good people," Martin Luther King, Jr. wrote in his famous "Letter From a Birmingham Jail."

So neither option is satisfactory. But what other options are there? That's a question that activists in Knoxville, led by members of an environmental activist group called Mountain Justice, asked themselves. By not assuming that the question was rhetorical, they came up with a creative and effective answer.

---

[15]I should note that "just staying home" is different from organizing a freezeout. The former is often an excuse for apathy. The latter is sometimes a very effective strategy. Activists in the town of Davidson, North Carolina organized an impressive example of this in 1986. When the KKK announced plans for a rally, students organized an activity day on the other side of town. They connected with local business owners and arranged for every shop on the town square to be closed, and for there to be no one there except for the Klansmen (the activists set up video cameras to document what happened). The Klansmen marched halfway across the square, then gave up and went home, since no one was watching.

I spoke at a similar event in 2013, "The People's Conference on Race & Equality", organized by a coalition of activists in Memphis, Tennessee, which happened at the same time as a Klan rally downtown (www.davidlamotte. com/2013/04/the-klan-went-home-the-community-stayed).

That day the Ku Klux Klan was met by the Coup Clutz Clowns, who had prepared carefully and found what theologian Walter Wink called a "Third Way"—neither fight nor flight, but a creative way to transform violence and hatred—in this case with humor.

When the Klan began to chant, "White power," the clowns pretended they couldn't quite understand what they were saying. They facetiously decided it must be a rally for "White flour" and pulled out bags of flour they had brought with them. A big flour fight and much hilarity ensued.

After a while, the clowns decided they must have heard wrong, so they listened again and determined that these strange demonstrators were actually chanting "White flowers." Fortunately, they had brought white flowers with them, which they then distributed to the crowd, laughing and clowning around as they did so.

When they had exhausted that gag, one clown pulled out a camp shower and the others tried to crowd beneath it, chanting, "Tight showers!" At some point, they started tossing toilet paper and chanting, "Wipe power!" Finally, they pulled on wedding dresses and crescendoed with, "Wife power!"

The Klan was stymied. Its members are accustomed to being feared and shouted at, but they had no response in their repertoire to a

The Coup Clutz Clowns in Knoxville / photo by Conrad Charleston

crowd having a wonderful time. They left an hour and a half early, with only one arrest—a Klansman who charged across the street toward the clowns.

As Scott Shepherd, the aforementioned former Klan leader who is now an anti-racism activist, wrote to me, "The Klan is successful with their public demonstrations only when they get the attention, feed off the hatred, and stir up negative emotions with the crowd. When the counter-protestors step up and take the control and attention away from the Klan, they fail with their attempt to get their negative message out. I have always heard that humor is the best medicine, and I believe this after witnessing the clowns' effect on the KKK demonstrations."

It is important to note here that none of these chants made fun of the Klan themselves. The clowns simply refused to take the Klan's ridiculous ideas seriously. There is a window, however small, for the Klansmen to laugh too. There is an invitation to transformation, not just a squashing of the opposition.

> There is an invitation to transformation, not just a squashing of the opposition. To move beyond the obvious choices of fight or flight, we must be creative.

They had found a Third Way— creative, nonviolent engagement. It was hardly an obvious response, but when they invested creative energy in the question of how to respond, they came up with an option that was more effective than the ones to which we usually turn.

The small Bavarian town of Wunsiedel is a point of pilgrimage for European Nazis, much to the dismay of its residents. Hitler's deputy, Rudolf Hess, was once buried there, but even though his remains have been removed, Neo-Nazis hold a march there annually.

In 2014, a group called Rechts gegen Rechts (Right versus Right) organized an involuntary walk-a-thon to raise money for EXIT-Deutschland, a non-profit that helps right-wing extremists find a way out of supremacist organizations. For every meter that the Neo-Nazis walked, local businesses and residents contributed ten Euros to EXIT-Deutschland.

As reported in the Guardian newspaper, "One of Rechts gegen Rechts' organisers, Fabian Wichmann, an education researcher at EXIT, told German news agency DPA: 'We want to show what else you can do, what other courses of action you have. You can do more than just block the street or close the shutters.'"

As John Lewis wrote in his book *Across That Bridge*, "Nonviolence is confrontational. It is not silent in the face of injustice, but 'creatively maladjusted.'" Nonviolence is not about passivity, but about being active. But to move beyond the obvious choices of fight or flight, we must be creative.

Artist Peter von Tiesenhausen was being threatened by oil corporations that wanted access to the natural gas beneath his eight-hundred-acre property in Alberta, Canada. Legally, the companies can lay claim to the land beneath private property, beneath a depth of six inches, but von Tiesenhausen didn't want his family farm, inherited from his parents, to be disturbed.

His solution? He created art across his land and copyrighted the entire thing, to a depth of six inches, which made any disturbance of the land a copyright violation. He also began to charge any oil industry companies that wanted to talk with him about his land a consultant's fee. "I demand $500 an hour. They pay. It keeps the meetings really short, and they don't do it nearly as often as they used to," the artist said.

Creativity is expressed through an act of creation. When we speak of creation, however, we tend to speak in scientific or religious terms (or an integration of the two). In both cases, we are generally referring to something that happened a long time ago and then was over.

That's not how it works.

The world is still being created. There is a blade of grass outside the cabin where I'm now writing in the southern foothills of Virginia that wasn't there a few weeks ago. Now it is. There is a flame in the fireplace that didn't exist two hours ago, before I built the fire.

And more importantly to me, there is a relationship being formed between you and me as you read these words. Depending on how long and how well we've known each other, that may be a new relationship just being created or an old one that is shifting somewhat because of this interaction, but regardless, there was a time before it existed and a time when it was new under the sun.

Julia Cameron, in her classic book on creativity, *The Artist's Way*, writes that "Creativity is the natural order of life." Life goes on, and so creativity and creation do too.

Ongoing creation is an everyday miracle that we tend to disregard. I should be clear, though, that when I say "miracle," I don't mean a case where the rules of science are apparently suspended and something entirely extraordinary happens. I mean that if we look at it closely, the existence and functionality of anything at all is beyond human comprehension. You, me, the laptop on my lap, the book you're reading—the atoms that constitute all of them are composed almost entirely of empty space. Yet you exist. I exist. We both think and feel and grow and hurt and heal. The words that appear on my laptop screen as I type today will soon be printed on paper in a building I've never seen, and eventually, they'll find their way to you. Tell me there are no miracles, and I will simply hold up a mirror. *Everything* is a miracle.

> Tell me there are no miracles, and I will simply hold up a mirror.

It is important, and sometimes difficult, to remember that in relation to a given problem, the possibilities are not limited to the possibilities we can see. When logic dictates that we have exhausted all possible options, it helps to remember that miracles are commonplace. The world is constantly surprising us, and not all of those surprises are negative. If you hold out hope and work toward a good outcome to a bad situation, especially without a clear explanation of the path from here to there, you are likely to be dismissed as an idealist. History, however, does not stand entirely against you.

In the summer of 2008, I was part of an Interfaith Peace Delegation to Palestine and Israel with a group called Interfaith PeaceBuilders, now called Eyewitness Palestine. We visited people and places along the spectra of political, religious, and cultural context, having earnest, honest, and intense conversation with people of wildly varying convictions. It gave us a much broader view of the histories, cultures, and conflicts that pervade the region than we would have had if we had only visited holy sites or only talked with people on one of the many sides of that complex conflict. We met with ideological Jewish settlers, Palestinian and Israeli students of various opinions and social strata, secular activists, and religious activists of various faiths. Each brought their own views and experience to an extremely difficult situation and helped us to understand their own suffering and that of the people they love.[16]

Among the people we met was a Palestinian activist in Ramallah named Omar Barghouti. He and an older activist spent some time with us, updating us on their efforts to put economic pressure on the state of Israel regarding its policies toward Palestine and Palestinians. In 2008, there was a fresh push in that particular struggle, and Omar was one of the early leaders in that nonviolent effort. He shared a lot of interesting, and often discouraging, information with us.

The thing I remember most clearly, though, was a story told at the end of our time together, sitting around a table at the Quaker Center in Ramallah. Someone asked Omar how he maintains hope in the face of such a long struggle with ongoing injustice and so little sign of progress. How did he maintain the energy to keep up his work?

> It is important, and sometimes difficult, to remember that in relation to a given problem, the possibilities are not limited to the possibilities we can see.

Omar is four years older than I am, so he was in college during some of the later years of the apartheid regime in South Africa. He explained that during his college years, he was involved with the anti-apartheid movement. In those days, South Africa's oppressive government had the support of the world's powers. The United States and other countries had significant financial investments in the apartheid regime, and it seemed to be in their best interests to defend the status quo. It was a struggle of the powerless against the powerful, and the only real thing the former had on their side was that they were right; the system against which they were struggling was indeed unjust. There was no rational justification for optimism.

---

[16]www.eyewitnesspalestine.org

Yet the miracle came. After twenty-seven years of incarceration, Nelson Mandela was released from prison. Four years later, he was elected president. The bloodbath of retributive ethnic cleansing that most people predicted would occur when the oppressed majority came to power never occurred. As history would have it, the idealists turned out to be the realists in this situation.

Back in Ramallah, Mr. Barghouti explained. "We see what happened in South Africa. No one can tell me that nothing can change here in Palestine. No one can tell me now that I am foolish to hope."

And what of the fall of the Berlin wall? Those who predicted German reunification would also have been laughed out of the room—until it happened. We should not allow ourselves to be immobilized by the apparent bleakness of circumstances. History has a way of surprising us.

> We have come to a time in history when we tend to equate cynicism with realism and hope with naïveté, but that is simply not accurate.

Rosa Parks, at the end of her autobiography, published in 1992, wrote with wonder, "Thirty years ago no one would have believed that Jesse Jackson, a Black man, could run for president of the United States and get White votes in the state primary elections."

If only she had lived four years longer and seen a Black man named Barack Obama elected president.

We have come to a time in history when we tend to equate cynicism with realism and hope with naïveté, but that is simply not accurate. College students, youth at camp retreats, people at music festivals, and others having "mountaintop" experiences commonly refer to returning to the "real world," as though these short-term gatherings aren't also part of the real world. But they are empirically no less real than anywhere else; and if they are especially nourishing and life-giving experiences for us, then maybe rather than dismissing them as unreal, we should try to figure out how we can make the rest of the world a bit more like them.

Twice a year, thousands of people gather on a hot, dusty ranch in Kerrville, Texas, for the Kerrville Folk Festival. For eighteen days each spring and a few more in the fall, music flows through sound systems on big stages and through acoustic instruments around campfires in the campgrounds. Longtime friends gather in makeshift popup tent neighborhoods where they have gathered for years and catch up on the year's news and a new crop of songs. It is a kind place, where eccentricities are at least tolerated and usually celebrated, and where attendees catch a glimpse of what a kinder and more tolerant world might look like. Near the front gate there is a sign that says, "Welcome home." Nearby, there is another sign that says, "It can be this way always."

This could easily (and reasonably) be dismissed as foolish idealism, or it could be embraced as a vision to work toward. The first step in changing the "real world" is to imagine a better way, but we tend to shut down the voices of those who articulate such ideas. "You may say I'm a dreamer," John Lennon wrote, quite familiar with the charge of being an idealist.

But perhaps "ideal-ist" is better defined as one who can envision ideals. That doesn't necessarily mean one who confuses reality with an imagined perfect circumstance. It can also mean one who is committed to moving closer to that better scenario. If we cannot envision a better way, we have little hope of creating it. The first step is the creative phase—the imagining; the second is building the bridge from here to there. Merriam-Webster defines the suffix "-ist" as one who performs a specified action, or one who produces a specified thing. So an idealist is arguably one who performs or produces their ideals.

Poets have been trying to get this point across for some time. Thoreau describes these two steps to creation: "If you have built castles in the air, your work need not be lost; that is where they should be. Now put the foundations under them." Emily Dickinson said it another way, "The possible's slow fuse is lit by the imagination."

photo by Neale Eckstein

Creativity is necessary in the pursuit of world changing. As my friend Dan Nichols sings, "If you do what you've always done, you'll get what you've always gotten, you'll be who you've always been, you'll go where you've always gone."[17] World changing is not a multiple choice activity. It involves creating more options than those with which you're initially presented.

Yet we often look at a big problem, can't see a solution, and throw up our hands. If no one has figured it out yet, we reason that we are unlikely to do so. But the truth is that people are discovering and developing new ways to approach problems every day. It might make more sense to look at a problem, gather people together, and make space for ideas to unfold. In order to be creative, we will need to invite that creativity.

The respected conflict transformation theorist and practitioner John Paul Lederach described his experience of creative and artistic moments in peace-building work:

> **If we cannot envision a better way, we have little hope of creating it.**

I have found that transformative moments in conflict are many times those filled with a haiku-like quality that floods a particular process or space. We might call them the moments of the aesthetic imagination, a place where suddenly, out of complexity and historic difficulty, the clarity of great insight makes an unexpected appearance in the form of an image or in a way of putting something that can only be described as artistic.

Perhaps we should explore cultivating more artful and creative approaches to tasks that we generally consider to be rational, like negotiation and conflict transformation. But beyond that, we would be wise to consider including art by its more conventional definition in our work of social change, weaving it into situations where we might not expect to encounter it. Art, as we generally think of it, has huge potential to shift emotional context and change the tone of a

---

[17]This quotation shows up in various forms, in various places, with quite a few different attributions. Dan has spent considerable time and energy trying to find the original source with no luck, so I'm quoting Dan's particular phrasing. To check out his music, visit www.dannicholsmusic.com

conflict in ways that rational argument cannot. In recent years, well-respected peacemakers and academics like Lederach, Howard Zehr, my former professor Roland Bleiker, and many others have pointed to the significance of art in peace work, and they have valid points to make.

They are not the first ones to make such observations. Back in 1926, the famed Russian actor and theater director Konstantin Sergeievich Stanislavski, the father of method acting, argued that because the best actors could convey their meanings clearly, even across cultural and language barriers, the arts are fundamental to peace work. "The theatre," he said, "is one of the best and principal means of bringing about reconciliation and mutual understanding between nations."

In 2006, twenty-five people, both Sunnis and Shias, gathered under a large tent in downtown Baghdad, Iraq, to share poetry. They had come at the invitation of Yanar Mohammed, a prominent Iraqi women's rights activist, who had a vision for peacemaking through poetry. Kim Rosen, the author of *Saved By a Poem: The Transformative Power of Words*, described the scene. "The Shiites sit opposite the Sunnis, thinking it will be a competition. But by the end of the event, all are embracing and dancing together—because the poems from both sides voice the same words, the same longings, the same wounds." In subsequent years, the event grew dramatically, and, according to the organizer of the event, "with this ball of magic being bounced from one side to the other... they all turned out to be on the same team!"

This shift can also occur in contexts that are not rife with conflict. At the first National Conference on Restorative Justice, held in Texas in 2007, I was invited to introduce the plenary speakers. Along with the standard speaker introduction, noting their qualifications and the topics they would address, the people organizing the conference asked me to introduce each speaker with a topical song and story. It was a delightful challenge and a fascinating strategy. Before moving into the scholarly topics to be addressed by leading academics and practitioners from around the world, we had a chance as a group to open our hearts for a moment, to consider why this particular topic matters and feel that significance.

And it worked. Once again, what seemed to be the least serious part of our work together shifted the mood in the room in ways that I believe mattered a great deal, putting us in the right frame of mind to engage deeply with the ideas being presented.

In another effort to approach a serious topic through art, I put the story of the clowns and the Klan to rhyme and began to perform the poem in my concerts. Then in 2012, I teamed up with illustrator Jenn Hales to publish a children's book about it, *White Flour.*

The book has gone on to have some wonderful adventures and has received accolades from people like Dr. Patch Adams, the real-life clown activist who was the subject of the Robin Williams movie that bore his name, along with eminent nonviolence theorists Gene Sharp and Johann Galtung. It received favorable coverage from the Southern Poverty Law Center and several other organizations I admire, and I have a picture of John Lewis holding the book and smiling. In the aftermath of George Floyd's murder, it was listed by *Essence* magazine as one of eleven books they recommended to talk with children about racism. It was even set to music and recorded by folksinger Rod MacDonald. It has had quite a life. The original clown action was wonderfully creative, and I can't help but believe that the story has traveled even farther due to its retelling in rhyme, visual art, and song.

> Creativity is essential to the work of positive change, and vision is the first step in that process.

As thrilled as I was by all of that, though, by far the most wonderful part of the book's story happened six months after it came out. In November of 2012, there was a Neo-Nazi rally in Charlotte, North Carolina, a couple of hours from my own home. The counter-protestors, led by Charlotte's Latino Coalition, dressed as clowns, brought bags of flour to the rally, and took their scripting directly from the poem. NBC News ran national stories on it, including an interview with a city councilman wearing a red foam nose.

The next morning, my email inbox was swamped with messages asking whether I had been involved in the protest, but I had had nothing to do with it other than writing the poem. I later contacted the lead organizer, and she confirmed that they had heard my poem and been inspired by the Knoxville clowns, just as I was.

It matters which stories we tell. If our actions are guided by our stories, then it is worthwhile to create and curate better visions within them. Creativity is essential to the work of positive change, and vision is the first step in that process.

Performing at the LEAF Festival in NC with students from the El Tejar music program in Guatemala/photo by David Simchock

12

Stumbling Toward the Light

We learn a lot from the mistakes of others, but even more from our own.

—Fausto Cercignani

I've been married twice, though both marriages were to the same woman and only a few weeks apart. Deanna and I decided to have two ceremonies—what we refer to as our introvert wedding and our extrovert wedding. The former was a simple, quiet Quaker ceremony with forty or so people, and the latter was a potluck, music festival-style affair for four hundred in the center of the Warren Wilson College campus, complete with Frisbees, bands playing all day, and a clown parade put on by the children of our friends. Literally hundreds of people contributed food, wine, music, and various other gifts to the event, in true movement style.

In the middle of the afternoon, we were ready to have the actual service under an open-air pavilion, but it was overcast and warm, and our friends were comfortable on their blankets in the grass and reluctant to come into the pavilion. Deanna and I were waiting at the campus gym to walk down together through the grass and into the pavilion, and we weren't quite sure what to do when our friends resisted gathering.

Then someone cued the rain. The clouds let down their precious cargo, and everyone dashed into the pavilion's shelter. A few minutes later it stopped, as suddenly as it had started. It was the only rain we had all day, and it couldn't have been better scripted.

We had decided that we would go on our honeymoon between the two weddings, but we couldn't quite decide where to go. There is no shortage of beauty in the world, and this was, we hoped, a once-in-a-lifetime trip. Which serene beach? Which glorious mountain range?

We were still kicking those questions around when Deanna and I ran into her friend Stacey, who had just returned from attending a language immersion school in Guatemala. She had stayed with a Guatemalan family and studied Spanish during the day at a school that she highly recommended.

Her descriptions were enticing, and Deanna said, "We could do *that* for our honeymoon!"

We chuckled. Then we looked at each other. "We could," I said.

And we did. We spent a couple of weeks in Antigua, Guatemala, a beautiful town largely populated with tourists. Still, even in Antigua, or Gringotenango as it is sometimes called, we encountered plenty of people who speak no English and plenty of opportunities to build our budding language skills.

We thoroughly enjoyed our experience, studying four or five hours a day with our own private tutors for two and a half weeks. We lived with a Guatemalan family who spoke only Spanish. Kids, it turns out, are excellent language teachers. They have smaller vocabularies, so they naturally start with the basics. They also don't mind repeating things over and over until you get it. They're used to it.

We spent our weekends on the more traditional honeymoon fare of Mayan temple ruins and a side trip to the idyllic Lago Atitlán, but we spent most of our time studying, and thus earned our lifetime nerd credentials by going to school on our honeymoon.

The school we attended, Probigua, used its profits to support libraries in rural villages. It also ran two mobile libraries built into school buses that circulated to areas that otherwise would have virtually no access to books. On Fridays, the school invited their *extranjero* students to come along on trips to those villages to deliver supplies, and Deanna and I were both looking forward to that trip on our first Friday there.

As it turned out, though, I got some sort of intestinal bug that took me out of commission on the morning of the trip. I encouraged Deanna to go anyway, and she had a wonderful adventure in the mountains, complete with the school bus they were riding sliding off the road into a mud bank, requiring all of its passengers to push to get it back on track. They took some paint, books, and a couple of computers to a library that Probigua supports in the hills not far away.

Back at the school on Monday, I was chatting with my tutor (and now friend), Claritza Morales, about how sorry I was to miss that opportunity, and she offered a possible alternative. Looking across the classroom, which is really more of a tin-roofed pavilion, she pointed out another of the teachers there. Claritza explained that the other teacher had a sister who taught in a public school in the mountains nearby, and she offered to ask her whether we could go for a visit.

I have never been as interested in tourist destinations as I am in cross-cultural experiences and in opportunities to understand what normal, everyday life is like for people. It is deceptively easy for me to assume that my lifestyle in the U.S. is a normal one and to forget that it is quite unusual on a world scale. Statistically, I'm an aberration in many ways, as you likely are, as well.

> It is deceptively easy for me to assume that my lifestyle in the U.S. is a normal one and to forget that it is quite unusual on a world scale.

Having multiple pairs of shoes, for instance, sets me apart from the majority of the world's population as relatively wealthy. Because it was outside of my normal experience and provided a glimpse of someone else's daily life, visiting a public school in a small, non-tourist-infested village in Guatemala was extremely interesting to me.

Claritza spoke with her colleague, who got in touch with her sister; and a few days later, we went into the mountains, up roads that were sometimes paved and sometimes mud, past burros and pigs, small houses and the people who lived in them, until we found ourselves in the village of Santa Lucia Milpas Altas.

The director of the school met us at the chain-link fence that surrounded the school and welcomed us. He was young, bespectacled, and professional. It was easy to see he was proud of the school, though his eyebrows drew together when he spoke of struggles they were facing, overcrowding prominent among them. A little way down the road from the school, only accessible via a small dirt path, there was a cinder block building they were using to teach classes. It seemed to be a house that was half finished, with several rooms inside but no windows. A single light bulb hung from the center of the bare room, with worn student chairs packed against each other along the walls. Someone had made an effort to brighten the space with some colorful cutouts of Disney characters and the word *'Bienvenidos'* in orange paper letters taped to one wall, but the tape wasn't holding on the rough cinder blocks, so the last few letters of the word had folded over and were hanging down the wall.

The rest of the school was in better shape than that, and, in fact, better than I would find at many other schools I would visit in coming years. Still, they were facing real challenges. As the principal continued to show me around, several of those challenges became particularly evident.

The school had 218 students. In addition to not having room for all of them, one of the major problems was the condition of the bathrooms. That was part of my tour, too. They had North American-style facilities, but they were in extremely bad shape, with some of the sinks on the floor and some of the toilets broken. That wasn't the primary problem, though. The real issue was that they had no running water.

Somehow the bathrooms had been built without tying them in to the well, which was about twenty feet away (and yes, uphill). The principal explained that he wanted very much to buy a pump and run plumbing from the well to the bathrooms, but that it simply wasn't in the school's budget. I asked if he knew how much it would cost, and he said yes, that it would be about a thousand *quetzales*. I did the math in my head (which is *never* a good idea in my case). Sure enough, I thought, I must have done it wrong; one thousand *quetzales* appeared to be about 125 U.S. dollars.

Having spent plenty of time, like many of us have, reading the news and feeling powerless to have any kind of positive impact on problems so large, I suddenly felt incredibly empowered. At that point Deanna was working as a public school teacher, and I was a folksinger. We weren't considered affluent by any means in our own cultural context—but $125? We could do that.

But how was it that there was no budget for $125 to run plumbing to the bathrooms?

That was the day that I began to learn about the lack of funding for public schools in Guatemala. At that time, the Guatemalan government generally only paid for public school teachers' salaries, and nothing else. Not the building, not the electricity, not the textbooks—which is why many Guatemalan schools don't *have* textbooks. The schools have to raise the money for the bare essentials from the parents of the students, many of whom are living in abject poverty.

In recent years, the government has passed laws requiring that public education be entirely free, but the increases in funding do not appear to be commensurate. This has had the effect of increasing the rolls at schools, but decreasing the material support per student. And schools do still charge fees for materials, uniforms, etc.

Of course, the needs of the school didn't stop with the plumbing. As we walked around a bit more, the director pointed out the two women who were crouched down by a well that dropped straight down in the middle of the school's cement courtyard, covered by a flat steel door. They were hauling water up and shucking corn to make food for the kids.

It turned out that this particular school had a much-coveted extra grant from the government to feed the children, the equivalent of ten cents per child per day. Feeding children at school is especially important because it provides an incentive for parents to send their kids. Many children in Guatemala do not go to school; their parents did not go to school, and they are needed at home to help with the manual labor of subsistence agriculture, weaving, or whatever the family's work is. It is extremely rare for kids to go to school past sixth grade, which is considered a basic education.

The women were preparing beans, tortillas, and *atol de elote* (a traditional Mayan drink made from sweet corn, corn starch, water, and sugar), using a small butane stove. They were working in a space the size of an oversized closet, with dirty walls and paint over the windowpanes. It was clear that the school very much needed a kitchen as well. I learned that $850 would be enough for them to have one. So a thousand dollars would take care of both projects.

I had spent enough time in developing countries to understand that showing up and passing out money can be much more destructive than constructive. I didn't pull out my checkbook, and I didn't promise to send money, but I did commiserate with the director in his frustration, and I did ask for his contact information before I left.

As much as my heart had leapt at the thought that I could simply take care of the plumbing issue, $1000 was a bit different from $125 for this folksinger. I could have written that check, and it wouldn't have bounced, but some other checks might have, as a result, when we got home.

> I had spent enough time in developing countries to understand that showing up and passing out money can be much more destructive than constructive.

Still, I felt the tug to engage, and I was eager to talk with Deanna about how we could help and how best to begin building a relationship with the school that would allow us to work together with some mutuality and trust. I didn't want to be paternalistic or propagate rich North American/poor Latin American stereotypes. And yet here was a very real need for some very real children. We were being asked to help, and it seemed that we had the means to address it.

These were not indolent, charity-seeking slackers, as people who are poor are so often portrayed. They were ordinary people working hard to provide an education for children in their community with meager resources and few options, and it seemed that a small boost could make a significant difference. Certainly, the hygiene of the students would improve with improvements to the bathrooms and the kitchen. That could have a significant effect on their health and therefore their school attendance.

And then it came to me—what I do for a living is travel around, sing songs for people, and tell them stories. What if I told people the story of this school and asked if they would like to help? We could use our own money to cover the costs of getting back down here and arranging the details so that anyone who wanted to chip in could know that one hundred percent of their donation was going to the project. That way I could spend my few hundred dollars on the plane ticket and incidentals and still have $1,000 for the school. I could leverage our donation into more resources for the school than we could afford to donate ourselves.

So I did. When we returned home, I told the audiences at my next few concerts about this school and its needs, and I explained that if folks wanted to chip in, I would take the money back and see the project through. At my first three concerts, people chipped in the money we needed. As I recall, there was one $200 check in the basket we put out at the CD table, but most of the donations were in small denominations. People would buy a $15 CD after the concert and donate the $5 change to the Guatemalan effort, or throw in the coins from their pockets.

It had been so effortless to raise that money, and we could already see how far it could go in Guatemala. So we began to dream a little. What if we kept going? There was certainly no end of need in Guatemalan schools. Why not keep it up and address some needs in other schools?

> What I do for a living is travel around, sing songs for people, and tell them stories. What if I told people the story of this school and asked if they would like to help?

I checked my touring schedule and booked another ticket to Guatemala for the first gap I saw, in November. As it turned out, the contact information I had for the principal wasn't getting me in touch with him. The phone number seemed to be wrong or outdated, and he had not given me an email address. I knew I could contact him through Claritza and her co-worker when I got back to Guatemala, so I just booked the trip.

I built in a bit of time to visit some other people we had met on the trip and contacted Dennis Smith, a mission co-worker for the Presbyterian Church (U.S.A.), then based in Guatemala City. Another mission co-worker, Karla Koll, had been living and working in Guatemala for years and knew my sister Margaret from seminary, so I got in touch with her as well on a subsequent trip. I also dropped a note to David Glanville, a salty and colorful ex-pat hotel owner I had met at Lago Atítlan. We had stayed at his beautiful *posada* on the lake on one of our two honeymoon weekends between classes. I told these new friends that I was interested in learning more about local schools and that I had a plan to provide some small grants. Each of them was appropriately cautionary and encouraging at the same time. All three helped to nuance my understanding, introduced me to other good connections, and have continued to mentor me through the years.

When I got back to Guatemala a few months later, I realized I had made a big and rookie mistake. It was November. Guatemalan schools run from January to October. No one was to be found at the school in Santa Lucia Milpas Altas. I felt pretty stupid, and my efforts to track the principal down were fruitless. He was out of town.

> Nino himself had only finished third grade, but he had an entrepreneurial spirit, and he wanted his own children and the others in the village to have a fair shot at school.

I was back in Guatemala, though, and had started to investigate these new possibilities, so I followed up with the other folks I was interested in seeing. One of the men I had met on our honeymoon in Santiago was an engaging Mayan man named Nino Tecún. When I made my way back to Santiago, Nino took me to his nearby village, Tzanchaj, to show me a small preschool he ran for fourteen children in a rented room.

The preschool-sized desks were crammed into the tiny space, and Nino explained that there were many more children in the village that would like to attend, but he only had room for fourteen. Nino himself had only finished third grade, but he had an entrepreneurial spirit, and he wanted his own children and the others in the village to have a fair shot at school. He had collected and contributed the money to pay a teacher to come teach the children; he had opened the tiny preschool on his own, without any government or international support.

Before I first visited Guatemala, I naively thought it was a Spanish-speaking country, but many people in Guatemala, especially rural people and women, do not speak Spanish at all. Even among the people who do speak Spanish, it is often a second language; Mayan languages are many people's native tongues. At that time, however, public schools often only taught in Spanish, so the Mayan children were at a strong disadvantage if they didn't go to preschool and get a start on Spanish. More recently, laws requiring bilingual education have been passed, but in many places, they are not enforced, or the indigenous language instruction is of poor quality.

On that trip, I started meeting with Nino and learning more about his school and how it might move forward to better serve his community. A year later, we had built a sturdy one-room schoolhouse for $2500, complete with electricity. Nino surprised me by naming it *Escuelita David LaMotte*, which is simultaneously awkward and moving.

The school has grown steadily over the years, and later, with a lot of people pitching in, PEG bought land to move the school across town, and other donors helped to build more classrooms and bathrooms. In 2021, the Rotary Foundation funded the construction of a beautiful new school building that will serve generations of children in Tzanchaj.

In addition to Nino's school, PEG has now worked with over a dozen other schools, libraries, and community partners in Guatemala, serving different needs in each community, based on the needs and desires of our partners and their communities and working with other organizations as well.

But what about the original school that inspired the project? My concert schedule was demanding, and it was going to be some time before I could return to Guatemala, so my next idea was to ask Claritza, my friend and erstwhile Spanish teacher, to go and visit the principal to discuss options. When she arranged a meeting, I learned something else about Guatemala that I had not understood previously. Culturally, a female teacher has a hard time negotiating with the male principal of a school. As Claritza reported it to me, the principal was happy to hear of the interest, but he wanted to add some things in to the project. The inherent power imbalance, due to gender, profession, and social location, made the conversation more of a negotiation than a partnership, so Claritza made no promises and went home.

In the meantime, more projects were emerging, and they were going beautifully. I brought home pictures of the progress we were making with Nino's school and others, and people were only too happy to contribute. Many people have a natural and healthy skepticism of large non-profits, having seen the substantial overhead that some of them support and how little of their donations make it all the way to the projects. But because Deanna and I were absorbing all of the overhead (and keeping it to a minimum), and because my listeners feel like they know and trust me, they were (and still are) wonderfully supportive.

We decided to pursue 501(c)3 non-profit status and put together a little organization. We chose the name PEG Partners. The acronym PEG stands for *Proyecto para las Escuelas Guatemaltecas*, or Guatemalan School Project. A 'peg' is also the part of a guitar that tunes a string, so that made some sense for me, sitting at the intersection of music and education. Tiny changes in the orientation of a tuning peg on a guitar can have a big impact on the quality of music, and the same idea holds true for our work in Guatemala. Small efforts have proven to make a substantial difference.

> My own cultural illiteracy and incompetence with international communication efforts had blown this project after I had invited other people to be a part of it.

It was several more months before I could return to Guatemala, but when I did, I made another effort to visit the school in Santa Lucia, only to miss the principal yet again.

I was frustrated. But I had set aside the money, and I wanted to see the project through. I talked with John Van Keppel, who at that time lived in Antigua and worked with an excellent organization called Child Aid. John has been an invaluable resource in this work, and over the next several years he also become a real friend. On my next trip down, he picked me up in his truck, and we headed for the school.

When we arrived this time, my jaw dropped. I was amazed to find that there was a whole new school there—large, two stories, and well built. Kids were running around, and workers were finishing up final bits of construction. A teacher came out to greet us and ask if he could help, and we had a bit of a look around. After the tour, I needed a restroom, and I found a beautiful and clean one waiting inside.

What had been done here was far beyond anything PEG could have accomplished, and I was thrilled for the kids in that little town. PEG doesn't have any turf issues; it was great that more had been done by someone else than we could have done ourselves.

But I also felt pretty stupid. My own cultural illiteracy and incompetence with international communication efforts had blown this project after I had invited other people to be a part of it. They had been excited to have this direct impact, and I had not managed to make it happen. The money they had donated would go to other worthy projects, but I hadn't delivered what I said I would.

As I look back, I wonder if ultimately it might have served the school poorly if we *had* come through. Perhaps the larger organization with better funding would have seen less need if those two basic problems of a functional kitchen and connecting the toilets to the well had already been addressed.

What I do know is that this initial project which never happened has led to dozens of other projects, including a literacy project in partnership with Child Aid that has touched thousands of children's lives, Nino's school in Tzanchaj, significant book purchases and other improvements to several libraries in various towns and villages, support of several different existing schools, teen mentoring programs, and even an impressive music school in the village of El Tejar, which we founded in 2007 as a partnership with LEAF International. My initial bumbling led to so many other good things. That was not the last time I fell down on the job, but it turns out that getting it wrong may have been the best thing I could have done.

> That was not the last time I fell down on the job, but it turns out that getting it wrong may have been the best thing I could have done.

As I mentioned earlier, there has been a bit of a trend recently of books critiquing aid work. It's a good trend in that there is much to be learned about how to do this work in ways that nurture dignity rather than destroying it on all sides. It is entirely possible to do more harm than good and to feed destructive stereotypes and practices that wound everyone involved, especially when we fail to keep in mind the values that should guide us and center the voices of people most directly affected.

My concern about the trend is that it will feed into the already powerful temptation to dismiss and simply stop supporting constructive efforts that are admittedly flawed. This kind of work is inherently messy. Doing it badly is clearly not our aim, but sometimes it's the only way we can learn to do it better. Accountability is good. We should not overlook significant issues with bad models of aid work. But our best response is usually to improve them rather than discard them, and to have realistic expectations regarding the nature of this work.

Beyond the glossy ads and fundraising letters, the best of projects has negative consequences and the worst likely has some positives. Because we want to minimize the negative impact, we need to study and consider our values, approaches, and methods, to listen more than we speak, to learn from the people with whom we are working—especially people who are generally thought of as being "served," and to engage with mentors who have deeper knowledge, history, and understanding of a given situation than we do, many of whom likely come from the "served" population.

> If we wait until we understand the issues, the people, the culture, ourselves completely, we will wait forever.

But then we have to show up and get to work. If we wait until we understand the issues, the people, the culture, ourselves completely, we will wait forever. So we strike a balance between due diligence and engagement instead of waiting forever to figure it all out perfectly.

Our ability to dismiss flawed (i.e. *all*) positive efforts takes us back to the two parts of the hero game: first, lionizing our heroes and dismissing our own responsibilities because we're not heroes; and conversely, discovering our heroes' human flaws and dismissing their efforts as those of as charlatans and hypocrites. We do the same thing with movements and actions that we do with individuals; and in both cases, we find ways to abdicate our responsibility to each other.

In her fascinating book *Being Wrong*, Kathryn Schulz writes about how we view our capacity to make mistakes:

> Of all the things we are wrong about, this idea of error might well top the list. It is our meta-mistake: we are wrong about what it means to be wrong. Far from being a sign of intellectual inferiority, the capacity to err is crucial to human cognition. Far from being a moral flaw, it is inextricable from some of our most humane and honorable qualities: empathy, optimism, imagination, conviction, and courage. And far from being a mark of indifference and intolerance, wrongness is a vital part of how we learn and change.

Blowing it is not part of most people's picture of bringing about positive change. We expect effective agents of change *not* to blow it. But all of them (and us) do. It is easy to dismiss our own capacity to be effective because we know how flawed we are. We often forget, however, that all of the people we respect and admire are flawed as well.

> It is easy to dismiss our own capacity to be effective because we know how flawed we are. We often forget, however, that all of the people we respect and admire are flawed as well.

Making a mistake should not be the end of your effort. It's just step one. It's part of joining the ranks of all people in every time and place who work for positive change. We all fall from time to time. But if we must inevitably stumble, let's keep stumbling toward the light.

III: What is Yours to Do?

13

Discerning Your Callings

I have ceased to question stars and books; I have begun to listen to the teachings my blood whispers to me.

—Hermann Hesse

I don't intend this book to induce guilt. Nor do I want to convince you that you're not doing enough. Instead, I want to clear some obstacles from your path if you're feeling a tug to contribute in ways that you haven't before but don't quite know where to start.

I meet a lot of people who are completely overwhelmed with personal responsibilities. If you have a sick parent or child for whom you need to care, or if you feel called to some other very personal work, that matters. If you want to see a world where sick parents receive care, and you are caring for a sick parent, you are helping to create that world in the exact way that I've been writing about here: you're making an incremental, undramatic, significant impact. If you can connect with others who are doing this work and encourage each other in creating better and more sustainable systems of support together, then that's movement work. It all counts.

I wear a necklace most days that jewelry artist Melissa Lowery made for me. It bears Gandhi's famous dictum that I quoted a few chapters ago: "Be the change you wish to see in the world." My hope is that hanging those words around my neck will remind me of that important wisdom.

Which changes do you want to see and be? You may want to live in a world in which people stand up for each other in the face of oppression. But if you also want to live in a world where people take care of their families in the face of illness and hardship, then perhaps your deepest call, at least for right now, is to help create that world by the direct action of compassion. It is for you and no one else to decide what you need to be working on right now. That said, if you are feeling a tug, listen.

It can be hard to speak of *callings* and *vocation* in a secular context. They are inherently spiritual terms, and though I understand them that way you might understand them differently. Whether you conceive of that call as coming from some form of God, destiny, or your own inner wisdom, I am convinced that each of us is called repeatedly, and that if we can be quiet enough to listen, we will hear.

> It is for you and no one else to decide what you need to be working on right now. That said, if you are feeling a tug, listen.

The following chapters explore some questions that I find useful when trying to discern what I am called to be or do in a particular time and place. Some may strike a chord with you; others may not. Ask what feels right and listen to what you hear. This kind of discernment leads us to the work that is ours to do.

14

What's Most Important?

We cannot declare a happenstance "just a coincidence" without looking at whether it corresponds to a theme or an issue in our lives.

—Gregg Levoy

I don't think that my friend Patrick was put on the earth for the purpose of telling me I'm not bad as a bar singer. But I have to admit that it changed my life back in the late eighties. His casual comment opened me up to considering new possibilities, and that led to a long and personally nourishing career as a musician. My career led to my meeting my wife, Deanna (at a concert), and that led to our honeymoon in Guatemala. Our honeymoon led to founding our non-profit, which led in turn to some Guatemalan children being able to read who might not be able to do so otherwise. That led to my being considered for the Rotary Peace Fellowship, which led us to move to Australia, then India. And now, it has led me to writing this book, along with many other outcomes. It's hard to overestimate the potential significance of a small action.

That said, I'm quite sure that the comment was not a hugely significant moment in Patrick's life. It was one of innumerable moments that had innumerable effects. I had a young woman come up to me at a concert at Hendrix College in Arkansas a few years ago and tell me that she was leaving the next month for a stint in the Peace Corps. I celebrated that with her, then she looked me in the eye and said, "I'm going because I saw you in concert a couple of years ago."

I don't know what her subsequent experience was like in the Peace Corps or how she touched others' lives while she was there, but I suspect she did some good work. She seemed like someone who would. I certainly don't take credit for her choices, which were doubtless the result of many other factors and decisions, any more than Patrick accepts the weight of my decision to become a musician. Still, it's nice to think I played a part in there somewhere. And it's good to be reminded of small callings and our ability to be what the songwriter Chuck Brodsky calls "each other's angels."In discussions of calling, it is natural to look for a Great Purpose in our lives. It would be wonderful to search for and discover a sense of Why We're Here. More than one best-selling book has been written on that topic. But here's a surprise: I don't think you have a calling. I don't think there is a reason why you're on the planet.

> "What am I supposed to do with my life?" is not really a useful question; the enormity of it is overwhelming and immobilizing. A better question may be, "What do I do next?"

I think there are lots of them.

That may seem like a trivial distinction, but it is not. Some people may seem to have a dominant wave in their lives, while others throw a lot of smaller ripples, but the search for our Life's Great Calling can easily become discouraging and self-defeating, in the same way that Hero Narratives can be immobilizing. It's too big. And it's too daunting. And it doesn't look much like my real life. It seems to me that biting off some chewable pieces right now is a much more productive approach.

I spend a fair amount of time on college campuses, between speaking and performing, and I often encounter students who are anxious about what to do after graduation. That's natural, given that it's the first time in many college students' lives that their next steps aren't somewhat scripted. As they plan those next steps, I love to remind them that they don't have to figure it all out right now.

"What am I supposed to do with my life?" is not really a useful question; the enormity of it is overwhelming and immobilizing. A better question may be, "What do I do next?" That's much more manageable, and much more realistic as well, given that the average person in the U.S. now has several careers over the course of their lives. Not jobs, but careers—whole different vocational trajectories.

Even a larger-than-life historical figure like Martin Luther King, Jr., didn't start off with a vision to lead the civil rights movement. When he went to Birmingham, Dr. King was taking a job as the pastor of a church, or "accepting a call," as church people put it. He showed up to do the work that he was called to at that time, which was to pastor a congregation. When Rosa Parks was arrested, fifty-one pastors met in a church basement to discuss how they would respond. The young Dr. King was elected to the leadership of that group, the Montgomery Improvement Association. He accepted that responsibility, and history took a significant turn.

But he didn't go to Montgomery looking for that. He was invited into that work, and he showed up, after choosing first to show up for the work of leading a particular congregation.

> Once we accept that we have many callings, and that we don't need to obsess about find our Life's Great Calling, where do we start?

Once we accept that we have many callings, and that we don't need to obsess about find our Life's Great Calling, where do we start? After all, we don't want to waste our time and effort. We want to have a significant impact on something that matters. How do we choose where to put our energy? Given the long list of issues and problems that need our attention, what is *most* important?

I have been in conversations where this question became toxic. People who are passionately drawn to particular work in the world naturally feel its significance deeply, and it is easy to round the dangerous corner of trying to denigrate the work that others are doing in order to demonstrate the importance of your own cause. It can go roughly like this (with, admittedly, a bit of exaggeration in this rendition... but not much):

A: So, what are you working on these days?

B: I'm working on women's issues. I can't believe there is still massive pay inequity for the same work, and that women are so under-represented in leadership roles, so that's where I'm putting my energy. What about you?

A: That's great, I guess, but I'm working on animal rights issues. It seems like it's more important to speak for those who have no voices.

C: (joining the conversation) That's fine, I guess, but with all due respect, poisoned water is an issue for everyone, human, or not. We've got to be putting our energy into challenging hydro-fracturing.

D: Well that's important too, I guess, but your local clean water issue isn't going to matter much if the whole planet melts because of global climate change! Isn't that a bit parochial?

E: People, we *don't have time* for the planet to melt! There are thousands of nuclear warheads rusting all over Eastern Europe, and all of ours are still set to respond on a hair trigger! If those things fall into the wrong hands, or some little wire falls against another one, it's all over!

F: And if we don't deal with gerrymandering and election integrity, we won't be able to deal with any of that!

...and so on, until they have worked all the way around the circle and get back to where they started:

B: And if we had more women in the conversation, maybe we could make progress on some of these issues!

Everyone has a reasonably sound argument. Each can present compelling reasons why their issue matters most. Those of us who are passionate about an issue or cause naturally want to recruit others to it. But it may not be productive or correct to assume that everyone ought to be on board with our issue. Looking at the list in the facetious conversation above, it would be tragic if everyone was convinced by any one of the activists! What if all of them decided to work exclusively on just one of those issues, abandoning all the others? Even if we ignored all of the issues mentioned above *except* one of them, no matter which one, we would be in trouble.

You may be thinking, "But if they're all important, do I have to work on all of them?" There is so much that needs attention, not only "issues," but work and laundry and family and rest. Our email inboxes are full of requests for one cause or another, and it all seems to matter, but we know we can't do it all. Where do we start? And where do we draw the line?

Noam Chomsky, the famous linguist and activist, talking with Bill Moyers about his decision to speak out against the Vietnam War, confessed his own reluctance to do so:

> If caring is equivalent to taking personal responsibility to work on every issue that needs someone's attention, we are doomed to discouragement, failure, and depression.

I remember thinking hard about whether to get involved because I knew exactly where it was going to go. It's the kind of involvement which only grows. There are more issues and more problems and more needs, and once you are willing to take what is clearly the step that honesty and integrity require and become involved in these issues, there's never going to be any end to the demands.

Compassion fatigue is well documented. If this is our context and our experience, it's no wonder that people grow frustrated and tired of activism. If caring is equivalent to taking personal responsibility to work on every issue that needs someone's attention, we are doomed to discouragement, failure, and depression.

It seems to me, though, that this is another place where a shift in the question might help. Maybe, rather than asking, "What is most important?," the more useful question is, "Which part of this is mine to do?"

15

What's Bugging You?

If you are neutral in situations of injustice, you have chosen the side of the oppressor. If an elephant has its foot on the tail of a mouse and you say that you are neutral, the mouse will not appreciate your neutrality.

—Desmond Tutu

My son's name is Mason. We named him that for a few reasons, but primarily because we hope he will grow up to be someone who builds, like a stone mason, rather than someone who tears down. The time goes quickly, as most parents will attest. He is now fourteen with a rapidly deepening voice.

Though he is changing quickly, it is still not hard to remember when he was three. As three-year-olds go, he was a gentle and easy kid, remarkably articulate and empathetic for such a little guy, and fun to be with. But still three. Much of what we think of as the Terrible Twos actually happens in the early threes, I think, in the same way that much of what we think of as "the sixties" happened in the early seventies. We're funny about time.

In those days, he had not yet mastered the skill of taking turns in conversation. If Deanna was talking, he would, in classic style, tug on her pants and say, "Mommy... Mommy... Mommy... Mommy... Mommy... Mommy... Mommy! Mommy! Mommy! Mommy! MOMMY! MOMMY!" Luckily, whatever he wanted to say was usually interesting.

Sometimes a calling is like that: it drives you nuts. And I don't just mean that it's persistent. I mean that it's annoying.

We tend to think of callings in grand, slow-motion, cinematic terms, with strings swelling in the background and a beam of sunlight breaking through the clouds. Burning bushes and mountaintops and such.

Sometimes, though, our proverbial pants legs are tugged by what I have come to think of as *negative callings* rather than *positive callings*. The latter draw you into something because it looks exciting or calls for your gifts, like my decision to have a go at playing music professionally.

The negative callings, on the other hand, are in response to something that isn't right. We perceive injustice and we feel called to do something about it, to engage in changing it. Callings can come in the form of frustration or moral indignation as easily as positive inspiration. Both are legitimate, although the negative ones can be a bit less romantic.

> We tend to think of callings in grand, slow-motion, cinematic terms, with strings swelling in the background and a beam of sunlight breaking through the clouds.

If you are old enough and were in the U.S. at the time, you may remember that during the run-up to the Iraq War, there was a proliferation of bumper stickers that said, "God Bless America." Denotatively, I can get behind that statement. It squares with my faith (and it is specifically a faith-based statement). Yes, please, God, continue to bless America—which I'm pretty sure is intended to mean the United States in this case (though I have met people from several other countries in North, Central, and South America who take exception to that usage—they're Americans too).

And that's part of the point. The statement leaves me uncomfortable because it is conspicuous in who it leaves out. Plus, it's not theologically or rationally sound to recruit God to our priorities. If we're bringing God into it, we need to go with God's priorities, which, according to my own tradition (and many others say the same thing in other words), include loving your enemies and praying for those who persecute you.

So a bumper sticker more in keeping with my faith would perhaps have read, "God Bless Iraq," even if we felt convinced that Iraq was our enemy, a conclusion I question, but won't take on here.

Of course, putting *that* on my car would have accomplished little other than supporting the local car window repair business. I was talking about this with my parents in their living room one day, and I said, "Somebody ought to make a bumper sticker that says, '*God bless every nation.*'" That's not quite as confrontational, and it might make people think about it a bit—maybe even notice the contrast between the two and consider to which of those ideas they subscribe.

Then I smiled and groaned, realizing what I had done. It's always dangerous to say the words, "Somebody ought to..." I realized that I knew how to design and order bumper stickers; I had done it before as a musician. Just like the "Let's Be Neighbors" signs, I heard myself say those dangerous words, and knew I had work to do. When we hear ourselves say that, we run the risk of remembering that we are somebody. And it is sometimes an indicator that this is ours to do. We are, after all, the people who perceived the need for it.

> It's always dangerous to say the words, "Somebody ought to..." When we hear ourselves say that, we run the risk of remembering that we are somebody.

My dad offered the wise amendment that perhaps the bumper sticker should say, "God bless *the people* of every nation," to differentiate between people and their governments.

I had the stickers made, gave a bunch of them away, and when I could no longer afford that, sold many more. Now I've distributed well over ten thousand of them at concerts and through my own web site. When another company called to see whether I would allow them to use the design, I said, "Sure, no charge, no problem." Mostly I just wanted to get that message out. I have no idea how many more they have distributed.

I don't know what effect this has had, of course, but I would like to think that it has contributed to some significant conversations, whether internal or external. If it resonates for you, then you feel a bit less alone at a time and place where your opinion is not mainstream. If it annoys you, vaguely or explicitly, you at least need to take a moment to consider why, and whether your logic holds up. That's all I hoped for, and I think it has happened. And it was born of my frustration. It arose out of a "Somebody ought to..." statement.

Could I have spent my time and money on something more important than making bumper stickers? Maybe. I'm sure someone could make a reasonable argument that I could have. I tend to think, though, that that was my particular calling on that particular day.

I would not have gotten to it by asking, "What is my Life's Great Calling?" Rather, I had to engage the question, "Is this mine to do?" Once I realized that I knew how to get bumper stickers made and that this was tugging on me, it was clear.

My sister Kathy has led an extremely diverse professional life, including being a professional potter, running a shoe store, and even working with me for a while. In her forties, she became increasingly concerned about and engaged with our broken legal system, particularly capital punishment issues. Finally, she decided that she needed to go to law school. She began Cornell Law at age fifty. She likes to joke that she got her student ID card and her AARP card in the mail in the same week. She is now a public defender in Asheville, NC, changing lives every day. That proverbial tug on her pants leg led to a whole career.

> The corollary question to, "What's bugging you?" is, "What inspires you?"

Of course, positive callings count too. The corollary question to, "What's bugging you?" is, "What inspires you?" What do you see happening in the world that makes you sit up a bit straighter and feel a little more hopeful about the human race?

For my mother in the eighties, that was Habitat for Humanity. She ended up spending seven years as a full-time volunteer, founding and chairing the local chapter in Roanoke, Virginia. It was a great deal of work, but it brought her great joy, and that chapter has now built hundreds of hundred houses for people with low income to buy at reasonable prices with no-interest loans. Habitat relies heavily on volunteer labor—hundreds of thousands of people pitching in for a few days of dedication and "sweat equity." It is a massive movement built from the accumulation of many people's time and energy, donated because they see something good happening and they want to be a part of it.

In response to both kinds of callings, negative and positive, the next question is, "What small thing can you do about it?" How do we move from applauding something someone else is doing to doing some of those things ourselves? Conversely, how do we work to impede the things that seem wrong to us?

Ask yourself those questions, not in the abstract, but specifically. What's bugging *you*? What inspires *you*? What small thing can *you* do about it? There's no telling where the answers to those questions might lead.

16

What Do You Bring?

Talent is like electricity. We don't understand electricity. We use it.

—Maya Angelou

So how do you go about making a difference?

Get a job working for US Airways at the Guatemala City airport. I'd say that's the best way.

At least it was in June of 2008, when I found myself delayed in Guatemala due to an equipment malfunction on a US Airways jet. Airplanes are complicated machines, and it is the nature of machines to malfunction sometimes, so I was grateful that we were delayed overnight rather than flying on a plane with a mechanical problem.

The timing, however, was significantly problematic for me. I was returning from a trip to Guatemala in which I'd traveled by all manners of transportation imaginable, from motorcycle taxi to boat to the back of a passing pickup truck to a "chicken bus" (retired school buses from the U.S., so named because you may well find yourself sitting next to a bag of chickens, and also because the bus drivers play chicken while passing each other on the winding mountain roads, getting out of the oncoming lane just in time, or sometimes almost in time).

I was planning to fly home to North Carolina that night, drop off my grubby clothes, pick up my suit and guitar, and fly immediately to

California, where I was scheduled to be a breakfast keynote speaker the following morning for the biennial General Assembly of the Presbyterian Church (U.S.A.).

Melissa Gutierrez, an employee at the Guatemala City airport, came to me at the end of a very long line (read: the entire plane) of unhappy passengers, greeted me with a smile, and proceeded to spend a full thirty minutes working on finding some way to get me to California in time for my talk. At no time did her good attitude waver, in spite of the fact that, as I learned later, she was on the end of a fourteen-hour-plus workday, and I had just watched her dealing with several extremely unpleasant customers who seemed to hold her personally responsible for the equipment problem.

When I began my talk in California early in the morning of the following day, speaking to a group of mostly church professionals, I started the hour I had been allotted by thanking Melissa Gutierrez in absentia and expressing my gratitude that not everyone who is compassionate and generous of spirit goes into the ministry. And I wrote a letter to US Airways. Most of the three previous paragraphs are taken directly from it.

Want to have a positive impact and make good things happen? Get a job working for US Airways. At least, that is clearly one way.

Or you could become a Certified Public Accountant.

At least that's one way. My friend Katherine Neville recently retired after years working as an accountant. She's good at it, and she had a business card that says, "account your blessings." She likes putting the numerical pieces of the puzzle together and coming up with something that makes sense and doesn't have any bits sticking out. Me? Not so much.

But I have a passion for Guatemalan children having a shot at education, and arts and healthy mentors in their lives, so I founded a non-profit, PEG Partners, as I recounted earlier. Because Katherine believes in that cause and has this particular gift to bring, she volunteered as the treasurer and CPA for PEG for seventeen years. She contributed immensely, and I can't imagine what we would have done without her. Now another friend has stepped into that role, bringing gifts that I simply don't have, and for which I am profoundly grateful.

I'm sure you see where I'm going with this. There are many kinds of callings and many ways to contribute. Two of the helpful questions we can ask ourselves to determine what we will take on have to do with what particular we bring as individuals. What do *you* bring?

That's a broad and general question. To narrow it down, ask a couple of other questions as well. The first one is, "What are you good at?" What can you do that not everyone can do?

The second is, "What do you love doing?" The answers may not always be the same thing, but they can both be enlightening questions to ask when you are considering your vocations (in the sense of "callings" rather than "jobs"). Your skills, whatever they may be, are needed somewhere. Really.

According to theologian and author Gil Bailie, the famed philosopher and preacher Howard Thurman once said to him in a private conversation, "Don't ask what the world needs. Ask what makes you come alive and then go and do it, because what the world needs is people who have come alive."

> You may be thinking that what you love has no place in service. If so, I would encourage you to think a bit more about it before letting the idea go.

I am surprised that, according to Bailie, Thurman didn't say, "Don't *just* ask what the world needs..." Having since read more of Thurman's writing I'm convinced that Thurman wanted us to ask both questions—what the world needs *and* what makes us come alive, and to look for the intersection between the two.

At any rate, Thurman was clearly pointing to the value of your own passion when it comes to the service of the world. You may be thinking that what you love has no place in service. If so, I would encourage you to think a bit more about it before letting the idea go. Our passion sometimes has potential for good that we may not see at first glance.

I got an email from a student named Eric Keen a few years ago. He wrote that he had seen a concert of mine the summer before and had been thinking a lot about some things I had shared during the concert, including the Howard Thurman quotation I mention above. Eric said that at first it hadn't seemed like those words applied to him.

Eric explained that he and his best friend Jason had a passion for cycling. When they weren't riding bikes they were talking about them, working on them, researching them, etc. Cycling is not a destructive hobby, but the primary benefits seemed to be mostly personal. Riding didn't burn fossil fuels and it developed their own health, but they didn't see a proactive generosity in it. How could riding their bikes be of service to others?

As they talked about it, though, an idea began to emerge. If they cycled across Canada and took pledges for their adventure, they could raise money, have a fun summer, and spend a *lot* of time riding their bikes. In the summer of 2008 they did just that, and they raised over $14,000 for a school in Chacaya, Guatemala, a small coffee-growing village on Lago Atítlan.[18] In cooperation with another organization, Sharing the Dream, the local Parents' Committee, and community leaders had raised money to buy some land and move their school out of a rented space with walls made of loosely woven reeds, and they had asked PEG Partners if we could help to build the school. Eric and Jason made a huge contribution to that effort, and had a whole lot of fun doing it. I have visited the school several times since then, and I can testify to the positive effect it has had for them to be in a sturdy, safe, and clean building. We sometimes think that if we're not miserable, we're not trying hard enough, not answering our most 'noble' call. However, I think Howard Thurman is closer to the truth: if our work is making

---

[18]Jason and Eric published a book about the experience: http://bit.ly/1kemtGZ

Dreaming of the Chacaya school, on the land where it would later be built

us miserable, it may *not* be our deepest call. On the other hand, if it is making us come alive, that may be a clue that we're on the right track.

That's not to say that good work doesn't sometimes require real sacrifice, courage, and suffering. Clearly, it does, and sometimes in large measure. Reading civil rights hero John Lewis' autobiography, *Walking With the Wind*, I find it hard not to be overwhelmed by the abuse that he and his companions willingly chose to endure in order to expose and challenge systems of oppression.

"Faith contains a certain ferocity," writes Gregg Levoy in his book *Callings*, "an unspoken demand that to maintain it we part ways with comfort and give up something we have for something we want. We may have to relinquish the precious commodities of time and energy, or something that represents security to us, or simply whatever internal resistance stands in our way."

> We should be careful to distinguish between the idea that courage and service sometimes require suffering and the idea that suffering is noble in and of itself.

Levoy is right. Sometimes world changing requires stepping beyond comfort and even safety. But we should be careful to distinguish between the idea that courage and service sometimes require suffering and the idea that suffering is noble in and of itself. Our joy can also be of service, and that kind of service tends to be more sustainable.

Lewis and his friends were willing to relinquish even their personal safety for some other things they wanted: freedom and equality. But I can attest to the fact that, even in the face of the great sacrifices he has made, Lewis' work unquestionably made him "come alive." He was always quick to smile and laugh, and no stranger to joy.

Looking for where your joy lies may be a good place to start in terms of seeking your place in the movement to make the world a better place. It is also important, though, to look at the particular skills and resources you bring.

My friend David Gill runs a camp on the outskirts of Little Rock, Arkansas. Ferncliff is, in some ways, a fairly typical summer camp and conference center, with a fishing pond, hiking trails, a swimming pool, and campfires. It is a beautiful and peaceful place and has given the essential gifts of rest and retreat to generations of people.

In March of 1998, there was a school shooting just outside Jonesboro, Arkansas. Four young children and one teacher were killed, and ten others were wounded. Though it is not mentioned nearly as often as the Columbine shooting, this was one of the first major school shootings in the United States, events that have now become almost commonplace. David Gill thought that the surviving children might benefit from a camp experience. He made discreet inquiries to gauge interest, made the invitation, and began raising the money needed to provide that service for free.

Gill assembled a team that included psychologists who trained the camp staff and counselors and were available to the students while they were there. The camp was a powerful and fun experience for the kids. It was not designed to force them to deal with their traumatic experience, but simply to have a healthy retreat experience, with appropriate resources available if they were needed.

After the first year, it was clear that there was deep value in this experience, and the various people involved decided to continue to invite these middle school children back each year until they graduated from high school. It turned out to be eight camps over five years. I was invited as a concert artist for several of those years, and one year I was asked to teach a creative writing class as well. I led a corporate writing process with the students that involved generating and choosing a topic together, and the kids chose to write about watching Saturday morning cartoons in sock-footed pajamas (the last generation to have their cartoons temporally limited to Saturday mornings). These kids were not defined by their trauma, and the camp was, to some degree, a vehicle for them to resist that definition.

Then the story took a turn that no one anticipated. In 1999, there was another school shooting, this time in Columbine, Colorado. Naturally, the children from Jonesboro were deeply affected by this news, and their response was to reach out to the students from Columbine. Adults helped facilitate a connection (though the idea came from the students themselves), and some of the Jonesboro kids, being among the few people who literally knew how it felt to go through such a thing, traveled to meet with survivors of the Columbine shooting. Later, they invited the Columbine survivors to be a part of the camp experience at Ferncliff, and some came. Eventually, the kids even invited children from Sarajevo who had survived the violence of the Bosnian war to join them as well.

David Gill set in motion an extraordinary cascade of healing influence in the face of tragic situations by bringing his own gifts, and the whole staff at Ferncliff offered the resources of the camp. Later, the Jonesboro students brought the gift of their own experience to the service of others who had been traumatized and were trying to heal. They brought their skills, their identity, their passion, and their history to their service.

What you bring includes elements of your identity, the various resources to which you have access, and the skills you have developed, as well as your passion. At other times, the gift you bring is not specific to you. In the Moral Monday protests here in North Carolina, what is often needed

> There are significant shortages in rural India, but manual labor is not one of them.

is simply more warm bodies standing together at the legislature. Just being present is a huge contribution. And though your joy can feed your work, I don't want to overstate that point. It's certainly not all fun.

My friend Hugh Hollowell, whom I mentioned earlier, spent years leading an organization in Raleigh, North Carolina called Love Wins that nurtures community among people who don't have housing. He told me the story of a volunteer who showed up one day, asking what he could do to help. Hugh asked him what he did for a day job and the volunteer responded that he was an IT guy. Hugh said, "Great! We've got issues with both of our computers! Can you take a look?" The guy responded that he would really rather do something else, since he does that all day at work.

Hugh, a Mennonite pastor, says that he almost renounced his commitment to nonviolence.

Apparently IT work was not where this volunteer found joy that day, but it was a skill that was desperately needed, and one that he had to offer. If he wanted to be of service, offering that skill would have been the best way to do it. Not for the rest of his life, perhaps, but on this one day.

When Deanna, Mason (then just turning one), and I moved to India in 2009, I packed my boots and gloves. Just a few weeks before, there had been terrible flooding in the part of the country where we were headed, and the organization for which I was going to be working, Arthik Samata Mandal (ASM), does disaster relief work as well as sustainable development.

When I got there, however, I found that most of the cleanup work had already been done. More important, I realized how silly I had been to think that manual labor would be a helpful contribution for me to make. There are significant shortages in rural India, but manual labor is not one of them. It's not a particularly strong skill for me at home, either, so why would it be the gift I bring there?

In fact, I found that what the organization needed from me was in another skill area altogether. Arthik Samata Mandal is good at the work they do, which has largely evolved from cleaning up disasters to sustainable development—making communities stronger in the first place, so that they can better withstand disasters when they occur.

They were finding it challenging, however, to tell their story, especially to Westerners. What they needed, it turned out, were some brochures. I am a decent photographer, and I knew enough about writing, layout and design to give them something useful, especially for a Western audience. They requested that I create brochures for three of their

Change Agent Training in Srikakulam for young women from nearby villages

flagship programs, so I designed, wrote, and shot photos to tell those stories and give the basic information and rationale for each. This served me well as field research for my master's program because I got to know those programs intimately, did a lot of travel into the field, conducted interviews, and shot over four thousand pictures, all of which was both academically engaging and a personal joy to me. I supported the organization in other ways while I was there as well, but the research, writing, and design were my primary responsibility.

That's not nearly as glamorous, of course, as slogging through mud to pull people to safety, but it was what was really needed from me. That can be another useful question to ask ourselves when we are trying discern calling. What is actually needed from me in this situation?

We have the same orientation with PEG. We try to meet real needs that are driven by circumstances in particular Guatemalan communities, rather than being driven by donor preferences. A few years ago, we helped fund a construction project at an overcrowded school in Pachaj, in the Quetzalenango province of Guatemala. We were originally planning to help fund the construction of one of the classrooms, but when the project began, the school officials came back to us and asked if they could use our money to fund a strong cement and steel railing around the whole area, something that would be a significant contribution to the children's safety. It doesn't sound nearly as cool to say that we funded the construction of a railing as it does to say that we funded the construction of a classroom; but that was what was really needed, and our goal is to be of real service, not just service that sounds good.

> Sometimes we are called to care for the people around us in particular ways that only we are suited for.

This question of "what you bring" came to me in stark relief this year when I was arrested for the second time in my life, as part of the Moral Monday movement here in North Carolina, again in the State Legislative Building. This time I was arrested for second-degree trespassing (in a public building), and for some version of disturbing the peace, which included "loud singing." I'm particularly proud of that charge, as I'm actually a rather quiet singer. I never would have made it in the days before microphones.

It occurred to me at one point how glad I was that my volunteer lawyer had not chosen to be arrested as part of those protests, since he would then not be available to do the work he was doing. I brought my part, and he brought his. Likewise, it is good that I was not called on to do his job, as I don't have a specialty in law. I'm also deeply grateful for the people who brought sandwiches to the church, where we all gathered at 4 a.m. when we were released, and to the people playing guitars, singing, and laughing in that fellowship hall. It was incredibly cleansing to have their joy and their music wash over us after being in jail.

But calling is not always about "issues," either. Sometimes we are called to care for the people around us in particular ways that only we are suited.

In the last few pages of Rosa Parks's autobiography, she offhandedly writes these words about the period after her husband died from cancer in 1977:

> Mama was ill with cancer too, and after my husband died, I had to put her in a nursing home for a year, because I wasn't able to give her the proper care and work too. But I visited her for breakfast, lunch, and dinner every day, seven days a week.

As she so often did, Rosa Parks sets quite a high bar for the rest of us, but I think it's notable that this deeply committed, legendary activist, named by *Time Magazine* as one of the hundred most influential people of her century, prioritized her family. There is no failure in that.

No one has the authority or the knowledge to tell you what you are or are not called to do. It is a deeply personal question, and it requires courageous self-examination and deep listening. If you are feeling tugged to engage in ways that you haven't before, to reach outside of your immediate circle of comfort, that may be something to which you need to pay attention.

The one thing I hope to get across in these pages is that the most significant work is often the least dramatic. Do the thing that is yours to do in this moment. And if your body and spirit are telling you that your highest call right now is to nourish and heal yourself, then please do that. We need you for the long haul, and when you are ready for the next thing, I trust that you will feel that tug.

You're still reading, though, so maybe you're already feeling it.

17

Personal Sustainability

To allow oneself to be carried away by a multitude of conflicting concerns, to surrender to too many demands, to commit oneself to too many projects, to want to help everyone in everything, is to succumb to violence.

—Thomas Merton

When I was a child, more than a few well-intentioned adults told me that if I worked hard enough and made good decisions, I could do anything I wanted to. I just had to set my mind to it and get to work.

This came as encouragement from people who believed in me and wanted me to believe in myself. These people didn't want me to be defeated by my own insecurities. They wanted me to perceive possibility for directions in which my life could go. They wanted me to dream big and go for it, because they cared about me and wanted me to live a full and rich life.

I remain grateful for that kindness and support. For there were other voices in my life then who were giving me the opposite message, and it probably served me well to be offered that encouraging perspective.

But it's not true.

For instance, even if I decided today that I am going to devote the rest of my life to being a professional NFL linebacker, it's still not going to happen. Even if I had decided that as a child, I still wouldn't have had an NFL career. I don't have the required genetic gifts. We all have limitations, and those limitations are as unique to each of us as our gifts are. They aren't flaws or shortcomings, they are just part of the boundaries of our being. Boundaries are not a bad thing.

I don't think those kind caretakers intended to lie to me; I think they hadn't thought it through. They were offering a simplified version of the truth, and—like the simplified version of the Rosa Parks arrest story—when we simplify a story too much it stops being accurate. We don't serve our kids well by telling them things that sound encouraging but aren't true.

The truth for which I believe they were aiming is this: Almost everyone on the planet, very likely including you, is capable of much, much more than we imagine. The main obstacle in our way is a belief in limitations that do not, in fact, exist.

That's a more complex idea, but it has the added benefit of being true.

Each of us has real limits regarding both our capacity for particular tasks, and how much we can take on at any given time. It is also true that if you take a step toward involvement in something that matters to you, it is likely that your awareness will increase, and you will drop some of your defenses regarding getting involved with *other* things that *also* matter to you. Before you know it, you may find that you have your time, money, and emotional energy invested in so many causes that you can't seem to remember the passion that got you involved in the first place. So how do you cope with that overload?

I've been happy to see the term "'personal sustainability" gaining ground in activist circles in recent years. It raises the fundamental question of how you take care of yourself so that you can continue to contribute.

That is not the only question, of course. You are also worthy of joy and rest simply by virtue of your existence, and not only because those are necessary for you to continue to contribute. I resist the personal commodification that leads to us thinking of self-care only as a vehicle to further output. Even if we allow that transactional view, though, there is still an important message here: to do this work well, we must invest in taking care of ourselves. What if we were to nurture ourselves for the cause, rather than destroying ourselves for it?

So when is the last time you felt some joy and peace and rest? Who were you with? Where were you? What were you doing? Whoever, wherever, and whatever those were, your homework for today is to put that back on your calendar. Not working is part of the work.

What Is Not Mine to Do?

The obvious corollary to asking ourselves which part of the work is ours to do is determining which part of the work isn't. That can be harder, given that so much seems both important and urgent. The best path I've found toward sane and sustainable contribution is to keep returning to the question of what is for *me* to do, rather than what is *important* in a general sense. This is a helpful part of discerning our callings—discerning where we are not called, as worthy as the cause may be.

When I am approached with an invitation to get involved with an event, organization, or cause, I have learned to ask myself several questions. The first is, "Does this matter?" In other words: Is it something I can stand behind? Is this effort likely to have significant impact? I think that's a good and reasonable place to start.

The second question is, "Are my particular skills and assets particularly valuable here?" In other words, are there other people available who could do this work at least as well as I can? That's sometimes an illuminating question, and it once led me to leave a job, because there was other work that felt uniquely mine to do, though I could think of several people who could do the work I had been doing as well as I had done it.

Now I am trying to learn to ask a third question, which is, "What and who will suffer if I take this on?" Given the commitments that I have already made, what will I need to pull back from in order to do this, and what will be the cost to that effort or those people? This includes not only my "day job" and my creative work as a musician and writer, but the time I spend with my family and the degree of attention I can offer them, given my preoccupation with other things. Those are important questions too, and I have often neglected to ask them.

In examining whether we should take on a particular role, it is also important to think about our identity and social location. Questions of diversity and equity require us to think not only about who is invited to the table, but who is doing the inviting. In a culture where people whose identities are considered mainstream (White, male, straight, cis-gendered, able-bodied, etc.) are often expected to be in positions of leadership, it can be quite powerful to challenge those expectations. If we care about equity and inclusion, that will sometimes require people who are mainstream to step aside to make room for other talents and perspectives.

Alexis Ohanian, the co-founder of Reddit, a social news aggregator and discussion Web site, resigned from the company's board on June 5, 2020, asking that he be replaced by a Black board member. Five days later, Michael Siebel became the company's first.

It can be challenging to step back when there is such strong encouragement to step forward and be a leader. Sometimes, however, the best way to support a movement is to step back rather than forward.

> The world may need a few martyrs from time to time, but very few.

If you are a part of a marginalized group, stepping forward can be costly and challenging, given that inordinate scrutiny and criticism will often be directed at you. Sometimes it may still be yours to do, though that decision is ultimately your own.

There is so much—too much—that is worthy of our time, but it is important to remember that time is a non-renewable resource. We have more impact across the span of our lives if we can stay in the work rather than burning out or damaging our health and close relationships through destructive patterns of overcommitment. That is not a justification for stepping back from all of the work, but it is an encouragement to prioritize.

We quite literally can't do it all, and the Hero Narrative works against us here. The heroes in our movies and history books often seemed to be able to do it all. It is another manifestation of the Hero Narrative to overestimate our individual importance to a particular effort. Stepping back from a particular role may leave some turmoil and chaos that look scary for a while, but people generally work things out, just as a river closes around a rock in its way.

It is also true that saying yes and then not coming through is a hardship on the folks who are asking you to contribute.

When a zealous friend is trying to recruit you to their cause, it's okay to say, "That's important, and I'm cheering you on as you work on it, but it's not mine to do right now. I am committed to some other things that are also important."

I recall offering some version of that response to a friend who was asking for my help within the last year. He smiled and said, "Okay. I'm an organizer. It's my job to ask, and it's your job to say yes or no." I think the conversation was refreshing for both of us, even though my answer wasn't his first choice. Burning out from overcommitment is not a sustainable or effective strategy, and seasoned activists know this.

Talking about booking concerts, songwriter Bob Franke likes to say, "'No' is my second favorite answer." Clarity is a gift. That's not to say that effective change work doesn't sometimes include real and even painful sacrifice and periods of hectic activity. As the stories of many notable world changers demonstrate, sometimes it does. If it is all sacrifice and no rest, however, you will have a hard time sticking with it for long.

The world may need a few martyrs from time to time, but very few. Personal sustainability allows you to *keep* contributing, which, in the long run, is better for both you and for the world around you.

18

The Power in Who You Are

So the rose is its own credential, a certain unattainable effortless form:

wearing its heart visibly, it gives us heart too: bud, fullness and fall.

—*Daniel Berrigan,* from the poem "Credentials," 1957

The only time that I ever performed for a fully armed audience was in Bosnia and Herzegovina, in the year 2000. At least that's the only time I am aware of. I have performed in Texas quite a bit.

I was heading to Europe for a concert tour, playing in a few European countries after concerts in Australia and New Zealand. Maryl Neff, a friend I knew from acoustic music circles in the United States, was working as a civilian employee for the U.S. Army, serving peacekeeping troops in Bosnia. Part of her duty included booking entertainment for the troops stationed on the base where she lived, and UN peacekeeping troops from several different countries often attended those events. When she saw that I was coming to Europe on a concert tour, she dropped a note to see whether I wanted to come perform at Eagle Base in Tuzla. In the aftermath of the brutal Bosnian war, that area was still considered a "hostile fire zone," so the troops were required to have firearms and ammunition with them at all times.

I tuned my guitar very carefully that night.

OK, I wasn't really worried that I would be shot. The pub on the base where I performed served only non-alcoholic drinks, so, as Master Sergeant Brian O'Connors quipped, "Neither the weapons nor the troops were loaded." I had prepared myself for some ribbing, however, stepping into a military culture with my long hair and bestickered guitar case. It seemed likely that I would have some stereotyping to contend with—and as it turned out, I did.

The audience was attentive, enthusiastic, and extremely supportive, all the while holding their rifles at their sides. After the show, several of us stood and talked for a while, and I passed my guitar around so that others could play a bit too. I'm still in touch with one soldier I met that night, who recently celebrated his retirement.

The entire night, there was not a single mention of my out-of-place hairstyle. Not one. I did have to contend with stereotypes that night, but not theirs: my own. My assumptions that I would be "othered" in that context were unfair and inaccurate.

Later, in Sarajevo, I connected with Dzevad Avdagic, a Muslim man who was working for the Christian organization Church World Service. Dzevad welcomed me into his home, and his kind wife fed me. I sat on his couch in the living room after dinner, drinking strong Bosnian

coffee while he told me stories. At one point, I reached up to put my finger in a bullet hole in the wooden frame of his living room china cabinet; the window had long since been repaired, but like everywhere I turned in Sarajevo, the evidence of the war was inescapable. Later, when we walked to town, we stopped at a red-dyed patch of cement on his street where Dzevad had held a young girl from his neighborhood while she died from a mortar shell wound.

Major Walt Spangler, III carrying my guitar at the Sarajevo airport

That evening, Dzevad and I attended what was easily the most extraordinary choir practice I have ever witnessed. The Pontanima Choir was rehearsing, and we stopped by and listened for a few songs.

On the surface, there was nothing particularly amazing going on; they sang beautifully, but many choirs do.

Knowing one incredible detail changed everything for me, however: These were Muslims, Orthodox Christians, Jews, and Catholics singing each other's sacred music together. In the immediate aftermath of a brutal war, with peacekeeping troops still on the ground and destruction all around them, these people, whose relatives had been killing and killed by each other, were standing side by side and singing together.

I can't help but believe that this courageous artistic act—intentionally re-humanizing each other, standing and singing together and honoring each other's faith and music—accomplished more than dialogue alone could have hoped to do. The members of the Pontanima Choir have made the intentional choice to open their hearts to each other when they lift their voices together, and the music they make is transformative. They have gone on to tour around the world, singing at venues like the Kennedy Center. They not only sing their message; they embody it.

> I did have to contend with stereotypes that night, but not theirs: my own.

Ivo Markovic, the founder of the choir, tells the story of its origins: "The idea was to be a form of positive provocation. We wanted to show these religious groups, so fully enslaved to nationalism, that there is another way to be, that religions can make positive contributions."

In an article about Pontanima, Andrew Packman writes, "Markovic's vision is for a living, breathing project of reconciliation. He believes that if people learn to sing the religious other's songs of lament, praise, grief, and hope, they will have come a long way toward loving one another. And if people hardened by the war can have an experience of beauty not just in spite of but based on Bosnia's pluralism, reconciliation might just begin to take root."

It is worth noting that it is the identities of the choir members that make this such a radical act. They are drawing on the power of who they are, and the beauty they are creating is enriched by their diversity. By throwing out the scripts that they are expected to follow as members of different faiths and ethnicities in a war-torn country, they are choosing to use their identities to challenge the very roots of war.

The closest I have come to participating in such an event was at the Abraham Jam concert I organized at Duke University in 2011. At a time when Islamophobia and anti-Semitism both seemed to be on the rise, the North Carolina Council of Churches, where I was working part-time, wanted to take a strong stand in support of our interfaith colleagues and friends. Students from all three Abrahamic faith groups and from several of the colleges in the area helped to put on the event, doing a lot of the legwork and choosing the name and the artists to perform. They wanted it to have high production values, so they sought out professional musicians. Dawud Wharnsby, a well-loved Muslim singer/songwriter, and Dan Nichols, a popular Jewish singer/songwriter, both joined me on stage, and I filled the Christian role.

> It was also an opportunity to build what we think is right, which is often the best way to oppose what we think is wrong.

Because, like the Pontanima Choir, we wanted to embody our mutual respect and support and not just talk and sing about it, we chose to be on stage together for the entire evening. We alternated songs rather than sets, and sometimes jumped in to sing a harmony, take a lead, or play percussion on each other's songs. We invited poets of the three faiths and a dancer to join us as well. The entire night was magical.

It was also an opportunity to build what we think is right, which is often the best way to oppose what we think is wrong. And it gave the community a different story to tell. That initial experimental event led to many more concerts. After a few years of playing together, Dan was amicably replaced by Billy Jonas. We went on to make a couple of albums together, as well as being featured in a short documentary, *Braided Prayer*. We performed around the U.S. and Canada, including shows at two different Parliament of the World's Religions gatherings.

Expectations are powerful, and defying them has the potential to shock people out of their assumptions. Billionaire Warren Buffet's advocacy for raising taxes on the wealthy, for instance, is surprising to many people and offers resistance to the temptation to categorize the 99 percent as good and the 1 percent as evil. We expect the extremely rich to be opposed to more taxes for the rich, but in this case, Buffet's sense of justice triumphs over greed. Muslims, Jews, and Christians seem always to be at war, according to the headlines, so there is a bit of extra beauty in seeing them sing together in harmony. As Richard Rohr famously wrote, "the best criticism of the bad is the practice of the better."

Johnny Cummings, an out gay man, serves as the mayor of Vicco, Kentucky, a rural Appalachian town of about 330 people. He has strong support in the town, which in 2013 became the smallest town in the United States to pass a ban on discrimination based on gender identity or sexual orientation. Stephen Colbert ran an ironic segment called "People Who Are Destroying America" telling the story of Mayor Cummings and Vicco, Kentucky, on his political comedy show, *The Colbert Report*. It made news because people from small Southern towns are not expected to be supportive of out gay men. It turns out that people aren't quite that predictable.

> Expectations are powerful, and defying them has the potential to shock people out of their assumptions.

My friend Imam Abdullah Antepli, of Duke University, is a courageous advocate of human rights for all. In the summer of 2011, he toured several African countries where there is extreme tension and frequent violence between Christians and Muslims. He traveled with a Catholic bishop, and the two of them gave talks and led worship together for several weeks. In telling me about it, Abdullah said, "Sometimes it didn't matter what we said. It was just being seen together on the same platform, treating each other with respect. That was enough to astound people and to change the tone." Who they were mattered as much as what they did.

So what is your own identity? Are you Southern? Are you wealthy? Are you an immigrant? Are you a veteran? Are you a member of a faith group? Are you poor? What do you care about that people might not expect you to care about? Where are you in the mainstream? Where are you on the margins? What tools does that identity afford you? There may be clues there to discerning what you might be called to work on next.

In 1982, when I was fourteen, I went to Haiti on a church mission trip. As is often the case with those kinds of trips, we did not make much of a meaningful contribution there in terms of manual labor, but we were radically changed—or at least I was.

My short trip to Haiti was the most dire poverty I had yet encountered. I came home painfully aware of my own privilege and the stark injustice of it; neither I nor the young people I met there had been given a choice as to where we would prefer to be born, but the random circumstances of our births led to much broader opportunities for me than for them. As a fourteen-year-old, I had a hard time processing that. I still do. It was one thing to theorize about it, another to spend time with real people who were just like me in so many respects— except that they were literally starving, through no fault of their own.

> I wanted to be in solidarity with the people I had met and had come to care about, though I didn't know the word solidarity at the time.

I have a clear memory from that trip, though I must admit that now, forty years later, I can't swear that it actually happened. It might have been a dream I had or a memory that has morphed over time. Regardless, the point is the same, and it has become part of my story.

One day in a market in Port-au-Prince, I became separated from the rest of the group (I am prone to wander). When I tried take a shortcut to get back to them, I saw a man lying across the little side alley through which I needed to walk. He was emaciated and appeared to be malnourished, though looking back now, I think it is also possible that he was racked by AIDS or another illness. The only way for me to get back to the group was literally to step over him. So I did. Even at fourteen, I understood the metaphor.

It is common for people to speak of such trips by saying, "I never knew how lucky I am." That observation is a natural first step, but it's not enough. If people who are privileged stop with feeling fortunate (or worse, 'blessed') because of that privilege and go on their merry way, there is a problem. To be honest with ourselves and each other, we must also acknowledge our common humanity, the injustice inherent in that unequal opportunity, and the responsibilities that come with privilege: a responsibility to work to open opportunity where it is lacking, a responsibility to share resources, a responsibility to listen and learn about privilege from marginalized people who are in a better position to perceive it, and a responsibility to subvert the systems that maintain that inequality.

At fourteen, I was troubled. I was ashamed of my privilege and of my identity. I didn't want to be White, or American, or economically privileged. Before that trip, I had thought of my family as lower middle class, but I was leaving out the world outside of the United States in that estimation. I came home and wanted to give away everything I had. That was problematic, of course, since I was fourteen and didn't have much. It's bad form to give away your parents' stuff. But I wanted to be in solidarity with the people I had met and had come to care about, though I didn't know the word *solidarity* at the time.

It was also a challenging situation for a fourteen-year-old, because I *couldn't* stop being who I was and still am. As someone pointed out in our debriefing of the trip, even if I had been standing naked and penniless in the middle of the Haitian countryside, I would still have been the wealthiest person for miles. I had U.S. citizenship, a middle school education, and access to higher education, White identity, and fluent English—not to mention that I was male and straight and a member of a dominant faith group, all of which offer access that is often denied, both in my own culture and in Haiti, to people who cannot claim those social locations. Though not from a family that was considered wealthy back in the United States, by Haitian standards I was unquestionably rich. I was dealt nearly the entire hand of privilege cards.

I have continued to struggle with this experience through the years as I've returned to developing countries and spent a bit of time in places like Atlanta's Open Door Community, which is sometimes described with a wink as an "unintentional community." The Open Door Community was made up of people who were formerly homeless and people who have never been without shelter, living in solidarity and community with people who are living on the street.

Spending time with these folks in Atlanta, I was able to process my struggles with privilege a bit more. As a teenager, I had simply held on to that shame until it soaked into my skin, but as an adult, I find myself able to look more analytically at these experiences.

It has been several years now since I visited the Open Door, but I distinctly remember a piece of art hanging on the wall not too far from the front door. On it are written words often attributed to Lilla Watson,[19] an Australian Murri activist:

> If you have come here to help me, you are wasting your time. But if you have come because your liberation is bound up with mine, then let us work together.

Those words speak to the fact that oppression damages all of us, even the oppressors. Though everyone does not bear equal responsibility, nor sustain equal damage, we cannot be neatly categorized into "victim" and "perpetrator" when it comes to social ills, and "helper" and "helped" are equally unhelpful boxes in which to put people. Pity attacks dignity; it does not support it.

Likewise, a sense of existential guilt has limited usefulness. Guilt is essentially self-focused; it emphasizes our own failures and inadequacies rather than directing our attention to others to whom we have responsibilities. In the short term, it may point us toward problems that need to be addressed. But if our sense of guilt doesn't develop into motivation for action, then it can just as easily be demoralizing and disempowering, convincing us that we are fundamentally flawed and therefore unlikely to have any positive impact. We are unwise to indulge it because it has an inertia all its own, tending to make objects at rest (ourselves) remain at rest. And objects at rest are much less likely to change the world.

I cannot alter my fundamental identity, even if I want to, and it is wasted effort to try. More importantly, though, changing who I am is not my goal, or at least should not be. My identity is part of the tool bag I have been given to do my work. Rather than wishing it were otherwise, it would be more effective to see how I can use this

---

[19]Lilla Watson, who has been, among other things, a professor at the University of Queensland where I did my graduate studies, does not claim authorship of this phrase, but says she was a part of a group that formulated it together. http://unnecessaryevils.blogspot.com/2008/11/attributing-words.html (note: this source misspells her name as "Lila" but the correct spelling is "Llla")

identity in the service of justice. How can I challenge systems that offer me more power than I deserve by working to support people who are unfairly denied that power? How can I use my circumstance of privilege to shine light on injustices and offer resources to those who need them? To use language discussed earlier in this book, how can I both work to meet people's needs and challenge the systems that make some of us needy?

I've tended to fit into the demographic mainstream for most of my life, but everyone, including me, finds themselves marginalized from time to time. Sometimes we find ourselves in both the mainstream and the margin at the same moment because we have certain cultural power by one metric and not by another. Both positions offer certain tools and certain limitations, and it is worthwhile to study them and come to understand where we fit in a given context.

I wrote in an earlier chapter about the night I spent in jail in May 2011. One of the reasons I decided to take that particular stand is that I thought I could contribute something simply by being White. The issues we were challenging that day included massive cuts to education funding, voter disenfranchisement, and the gutting of the Racial Justice Act, all of which have clear connections to issues of race and racism. In the subtle political landscape of North Carolina, some might have found it easy to dismiss my courageous Black colleagues as playing some kind of racial politics in their opposition to these policies. It was slightly harder to do that because Rob Stephens, a White man who worked for the NAACP at the time, and I were among the "Statehouse Seven." The makeup of our group showed visually that this wasn't just a "Black issue"; it was a justice issue.

> How can I challenge systems that offer me more power than I deserve by working to support people who are unfairly denied that power?

I don't want to exaggerate the significance of that contribution. Rob and I were followers in that group, not leaders. Rev. Barber mentioned our diversity as something that was good about our group, though, and I'm glad we could provide it. Identity should never be a basis for one person to be valued more highly than another, but it is unwise to neglect its tactical significance and the particular tools it offers. It also can be helpful in determining what is specifically ours to do.

In my case, I was also keenly aware that I have an audience as a musician, many of whom would be surprised to find that I had been arrested and would want to know why. That was precisely our goal—to get the word out about some terrible things that were going on in the legislature, and to give people a reason to pay attention and learn for themselves what was happening. When I added those things up, this work seemed as if it was mine to do, though I wasn't eager to do it.

Sometimes, our callings sneak up on us. Abby Goldberg struggled for some time to come up with a seventh-grade school project, until one day, she says, the idea hit her in the face—literally; a plastic bag from a nearby garbage dump blew up on a windy day and ran right into her. She started to investigate one-use plastic shopping bags and became increasingly disturbed by what she found. As an animal lover, she recoiled at images of sea animals tangled in them. Doing her own field study, she counted 173 bags leaving just one checkout aisle in her local grocery store in a two-hour period. Abby had a great idea for her school project: she would get her town to ban plastic bags.

> I was also keenly aware that I have an audience as a musician, many of whom would be surprised to find that I had been arrested and would want to know why.

When her research led her to discover a bill moving through her state legislature, though, she got mad. The bill would *ban* municipalities from *banning* plastic bags, while requiring them to meet very low standards of recycled content in those bags, thus enabling them to pitch the bill as an environmental initiative, deceptively calling it the 'Plastic Bag and Film Recycling Act.'

Abby's response was not what you might expect from a twelve-year-old. She started an online petition to the governor, asking him to veto the bill when it reached his desk. More than 174,000 people signed that petition, myself included. The petition got significant press coverage, and as more people learned what was in the bill, public opposition naturally grew.

The governor called Abby at home one night, just as she was going to sleep, to tell her that he had decided to veto the bill, and to thank her. Not bad for a seventh grader.

Abby's story is extremely compelling, and she would be an impressive young woman regardless of her age, but her youth is a significant part of this story. When I asked her what effect her age has had on her activism, she said, "I tell other kids to use being a kid to their advantage. We know a lot about social media, we have lots of friends, and we have time to get involved. Actually, I think it is our job to tell the adults about problems in the world. Sometimes adults are too busy to see all the problems."

On the other end of the age spectrum we find the Raging Grannies, who are often found at various protests singing well-known melodies with brand new, self-penned words with great passion and conviction. They are a group of older women, and most of them really are grandmothers. Their activism seems somewhat surprising because they don't fit our stereotypes of what activists look like. They make headlines both because they are adorable and because they are surprising, thereby getting the word out about the important things they stand for, and sometimes against.

> In that case, my nationality was significant. They needed to know that there were dissenting voices here in the United States.

I co-billed with a group of Raging Grannies at a peace conference in Berlin on the third anniversary of the launch of the Iraq war. I had been invited to speak to German peace activists because I was a peace activist in the U.S. The Europeans I met on that trip were not seeing anything in their media about a peace movement in the United States, so they were amazed to learn that there was one. In that case, my nationality was significant. They needed to know that there were dissenting voices here in the United States.

Closer to home, my father was arrested in the Moral Monday movement here in North Carolina shortly after I was. At that time, he was an eighty-one-year-old retired Presbyterian pastor, well respected and dignified, with no previous history of civil disobedience. He felt compelled by his faith to take that stand due to biblical teachings about defending and caring for the poor, who were, and still are, under assault by our state government. I wrote a blog post about his arrest called "*Taking My Dad to Jail for Father's Day*," and it remains the most widely read page in the history of the NC Council of Churches Web site. Lots of people know retired ministers; very few of us expect them to get arrested. Because of who he is, my dad's story resonated with a lot of people.

As I write this, my eyes wander up to the bookshelf in my friend's beautiful cabin where I am writing, and they fall on bell hooks's book *Ain't I A Woman.* It is titled after Sojourner Truth's famous speech in 1852, where, as hooks puts it, she "became one of the first feminists to call their attention to the lot of the female black slave woman who, compelled by circumstance to labor alongside black men, was a living embodiment of the truth that women could be the world-equals of men." She was a "living embodiment" of the story she told. Her identity was fundamental to her ideas and her efficacy in sharing them so persuasively.

> She had a sense of moral obligation. It was not only her country doing this, it was her own small town. In fact, it was people she knew.

My friend Allyson Caison lives in Johnston County, North Carolina. Sitting around a Boy Scout campfire in the late nineties, she first learned of a company called Aero Contractors, which flew "extraordinary rendition" flights for the CIA from her local rural airport.[20]

From Johnston County, planes flew all over the world, nabbing terror suspects, chaining them to the floor, and flying them to countries where they could be tortured and interrogated without any legal process or charges being filed. Allyson did not think this was right, and she was deeply troubled that these flights were based right in her backyard.

---

[20]For more on this, read Stephen Grey's book, Ghost Plane.

As she probed further into this, she was dismayed to discover that two of the principal players at Aero were parents of her children's friends. She knew them well.

Allyson is a real estate agent, and it would have been reasonable for her to demur, thinking that stirring the political pot in her small town could ruin her business. But she had a sense of moral obligation. It was not only her country doing this, it was her own small town. In fact, it was people she knew.

Allyson became involved with an organization called North Carolina Stop Torture Now, which is led by a courageous and knowledgeable woman named Christina Cowger. They organized a small vigil in October of 2007, and Allyson was in charge of acquiring permits. There were plenty of hoops to jump through, and she encountered open hostility and resistance among some of the town's leadership. It was an extremely stressful time for her. In the end, though, the organization held the event.

That early vigil led to further actions and protests, and over the years, the issue has moved further into the mainstream. Allyson, Christina, and others have appeared before the County Commissioners on many, many occasions, expressing their concerns. At one such meeting, Allyson read an entire letter by Anna Britel, the wife of rendition and torture survivor Kassim Britel. She told me that she broke out in hives from anxiety, but she still read the letter. She needed them to understand the humanity of the victims. It has been a long, slow process, as effective activism usually is, but ultimately, it is working.

The way Allyson puts it, "When you first start filling a bucket one drop at a time, for a long time you can't even perceive that the bucket has any drops in it (it's a big bucket). But eventually, one small drop at a time, it fills up and goes over the top. So each small act of kindness on behalf of the world's most vulnerable adds to the great bucket. And we will tip to goodness—I believe that with my whole heart."

By the way, it seems important to note that Allyson was later voted Realtor of the Year by the Johnston County Realtors Association. Apparently, her activism has not damaged the respect her peers have for her or her business, but if it had, she would have done it anyway.

As you consider what you are called to do in the world, it may be useful to consider what role your identity might play in your contributions. There may be road signs in the answers to these questions: Who are you? Where are you from? Who do you represent? How do others see you? What do you care about that people might not expect you to care about? What do you bring because of who you are?

19

The Not-So-Radical Activist

We cannot do everything, and there is a sense of liberation in realizing that. This enables us to do something, and to do it very well.

—Bishop Ken Untener, *The Prayer of Oscar Romero*

Earlier in this book you read about Jo Ann Robinson, who, along with two of her students, stayed up all night after Rosa Parks was arrested, making copies of a bus boycott flyer to be distributed around Montgomery. Robinson's book, *The Montgomery Bus Boycott and the Women Who Started It*, goes on to describe a meeting the next day with the principal of the college where she taught, Alabama State University.

After she finished teaching an 8 a.m. class, she left with the two students to deposit the flyers at designated drop points, where members and friends of the Women's Political Council would pick them up and distribute them further.

But when she returned to campus to teach her 2 p.m. class, she found a note from Dr. H. Councill Trenholm, the president of the college, asking her to come to his office immediately. Another teacher had brought a copy of the flyer to President Trenholm, and Robinson writes that when she entered his office, he was "very angry and visibly shaken." He told her that he had sent another teacher to cover her class, and he demanded an explanation.

Ms. Robinson's book clearly demonstrates her deep respect for President Trenholm. He had taken over when the school was a tiny junior college and, through deep investment of time, effort, and sometimes even his own money, had grown it into a successful senior college with a large and growing enrollment. He had engaged with the community, offering scholarships to needy and promising prospective students and earning the trust and investment of the business community.

During that meeting, Robinson writes, she was aware that she might lose her job but she was willing to do so. She informed President Trenholm of Rosa Parks's arrest and the circumstances surrounding it, and the earlier arrest of Claudette Colvin, a local teenager, in a similar situation. She described the outrageous and frequent ill treatment of Black women and men on the public buses. She told him that she had calculated the costs of the paper they had used for the flyers, and that the Women's Political Council would reimburse the school in full (actually, the WPC had no treasury. She paid that bill personally).

> Was this a hypocritical cop-out or the strategic wisdom of a committed supporter who rightly perceived his particular role and contribution?

He stopped her frequently and asked further questions. Robinson wrote, "As I talked, I could see the anger slowly receding from his face and heard his tone of voice softening."

When he had asked all that he needed to, and she had answered, they both sat quietly for a time. At the end of that silence, although Robinson writes that, "He seemed to have aged years in the brief span of our conversation," Trenholm finally spoke, "Your group must continue to press for civil rights."

He also cautioned her, however, not to neglect her responsibilities as a faculty member, to be careful to stay out of the limelight, and not to involve the college in the movement.

It would be easy to cast that last speech as pretty lukewarm, or even complicit with the system of oppression that they were enduring.

While people all over Montgomery were ramping up to engage in this boycott, which would be extremely dangerous for them, Dr. Trenholm's response was to ask Jo Ann Robinson to be less visible and to make sure she didn't involve the college? People were risking violence and loss of jobs (and therefore family income), and he was worried about his school's reputation?

That's not how Jo Ann Robinson saw it, though, and she offers this further perspective:

> Dr. Trenholm did not participate personally in the boycott, but he was mentally and spiritually involved—and deeply so! He was financially involved, too, and often contributed to the collections for people who were suffering because of the loss of their jobs... As we will see, once the battle was begun, the bus company and city officials would request Dr. Trenholm to sit on a board with them to help arrive at a satisfactory conclusion of the boycott.

Providing a principled and knowledgeable voice at the table in those negotiations was certainly an important role to play, and Dr. Trenholm could not have done it if he had lost his position at the college due to being too publicly radical, or if he had been branded as radical by the town's White leadership and consequently had not been invited to their conversations. Likewise, he could not have provided the desperately needed financial support he did if he were out of work. He needed to be a moderate voice publicly in order to support the cause in significant ways that no one else could offer.

This story, like all stories, is open to interpretation. Was this a hypocritical cop-out or the strategic wisdom of a committed supporter who rightly perceived his particular role and contribution?

It seems to me that there is often an unspoken assumption that the most radical and outspoken activists are the most deeply committed and important for a cause, but I don't think history bears that out.

My friend and mentor Dan Buttry, whose actual job title before his recent retirement was "Global Consultant for Peace," introduced me to a tool called the Spectrum of Allies, created by George Lakey and used by Training for Change in their workshops.

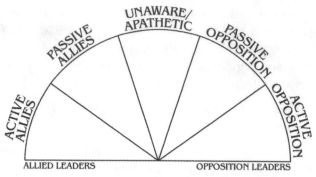

Spectrum of Allies

The Spectrum of Allies is a tool for considering a possible action and what effect it might have, looking at whether it is more likely to help achieve your goals or backfire. It plots all of the stakeholders in a given conflict along a graph, categorizing them as 1) active allies, 2) passive allies, 3) unaware/apathetic, 4) passive opposition, or 5) active opposition.

To shift the trajectory of a large group—like a nation, for instance—a whole lot of people need to move a little bit. The ideal action would turn your active opponents into passive opponents, your passive opponents neutral, some neutral people into passive allies, and some passive allies into active allies—though in the real world one action seldom has that entire effect.

In an election, it is really just the shift in the middle of the spectrum that usually results in a policy change, but in terms of large societal transformations, each of those shifts counts for a great deal. It is possible for someone to move in one dramatic shift from active opponent to active ally, but that kind of radical shift is extremely unusual, and is not necessary to achieve meaningful change. Every little move is significant, from any of those categories into the adjacent one.

This is what happened when Rosa Parks was arrested. The nation saw a dignified, non-threatening (challenging prevalent stereotypes) woman arrested for refusing to give up a seat for which she had paid.

This clear injustice caused some people who had been passively sympathetic to the cause of racial equality to get involved and become active, some people who had simply accepted the status quo as "the way things are" to become passively sympathetic to the protestors, and some who had been passively supportive of segregation and inequality to question themselves and move toward neutrality. Perhaps it even led some who had been actively involved in oppression to become less active.

I don't want to oversimplify the story. There were doubtless others who had been passively opposed to the aims of the boycott who became more active in their opposition as they saw their privilege threatened. When injustice is challenged, some sort of backlash is almost inevitable. On the whole, though, this action shook people from their assumptions and caused them to reevaluate. Though this work is ongoing, this was a notable period of progress. Through this and other actions, much of the nation gradually perceived the everyday injustice in which we were participating, became increasingly uncomfortable with it, and shifted sympathies, then policies.

> We mustn't dismiss the small efforts of people around us, or our own. It's not just that they matter, they are often essential.

This perspective further challenges the maximalist assumption above that more dramatic and radical acts and actors count more. If large-scale change requires subtle shifts all along the spectrum, then the most outspoken activists are *not* necessarily the most important or effective in a movement. Everyone on the graph has the best chance of influence on the adjacent pie slices and their own, and motivating the moderately sympathetic to become active, or the moderately opposed to become more neutral, can be a decisive shift for a movement.

Activists who are deep into a movement for a particular cause sometimes forget this and dismiss the small efforts and sympathies of people who are, in fact, our allies—or could be, if we would offer them a path. I have heard the clever insult "slacktivist" applied to people who rant online and click petitions, but don't show up for community organizing. This "calling out" of activists who are not judged to be doing enough is not nearly as effective as "calling in" to more engaged participation.

Worse yet, we sometimes impose these litmus test judgments on our own efforts, feeling ineffectual or weak because, for instance, we don't have bold enough bumper stickers on our cars, don't fill our social media with political stances, haven't marched in the streets, or haven't been to jail.

Sometimes a bumper sticker can provoke a good conversation, but sometimes it can prevent one. Sometimes marching in the streets is extremely important, but it may be that it is not your most useful way to contribute. Sometimes civil disobedience is a good tactic, sometimes it is merely self-congratulatory, a personal badge rather than a public service.

Because large changes require small shifts all along the spectrum, however, we mustn't dismiss the small efforts of people around us, or our own. It's not just that they matter; they are often essential. Once more, the question is not, "Am I doing enough?" but rather, "Am I doing what is mine to do?" So what *is* yours to do? It's time to turn our attention to that question and to a series of smaller questions that may help lead us to some of its answers.

IV: Pick One

"One cannot level one's moral lance at every evil in the universe. There are just too many of them. But you can do something, and the difference between doing something and doing nothing is everything."

—Daniel Berrigan

Having established that big changes are made up of small ones, that movements matter more than heroes in making change, that effective activism can take many forms (including not-so-radical ones), that real change is made by imperfect people, that hope and love are choices rather than circumstances, that world changing requires creativity (and that there are often more options than the options we can see), that our own gifts may have as much to do with our callings as the condition of the world around us, that we have many callings, not just one big one... having established all that, there's one more question to ask:

What will you do about it?

This final section of this book walks you through some simple questions in an effort to help you determine what may be calling to you next. I have spaced them out so that you can flip the page and answer each in turn. This exercise works best if you don't look ahead but answer each question in turn before moving on to the next.

The most important thing to remember in this exercise is that we are not trying to discern your Calling with a big *C*. This is not intended to help you figure out what to do with your *Life*, only what small effort might be calling to you *now*.

With that in mind, I suggest that you write down the very first thing that comes to your mind in response to each of these questions. Don't think about it too much. Don't look for your *best* answer, just give your *first* answer. You can always go back and do it again.

If you prefer to do this digitally, you can go to PickOne.org, which will ask you the same questions and give you a chance to share your answers with others if you like (or to keep them private if you don't, but you can commit to yourself and get a reminder email later to see how it's going). You can also read what others are up to, which you may find inspiring.

Ready? Get a pen, then turn the page!

Care:

What matters to you?

What is one thing that is driving you nuts? Put otherwise, on any scale from family to planetary, what is it that you just can't believe people are allowing to happen? What doesn't seem right to you?

Or, if you would rather answer this question: What really excites you? What are people doing that really makes you sit up straighter and believe in humanity?

Remember, give your first thought, not your best answer. You have many callings, and the question on the table is not what you will do with your life, but what you will do next.

Contribute:

What do you bring that not everyone can bring?

What do you love doing? What are you good at?

My wife, Deanna, introduced me to a useful tool for considering what resources you bring. Draw a four-box graph, and consider Gifts of the Head: things you know about, Gifts of the Heart: things you are passionate about, Gifts of the Hands: physical things you are good at making, fixing, etc., and Gifts of the Hive: communities you are connected to that you may be able to draw on to support your work.

This is not a time for humility, at least in the misguided, commonly understood sense of refusing to acknowledge your strengths. Be honest with yourself. What are your gifts?

HEAD	HEART
HANDS	HIVE

Connect:

Where can you find a community of people who are also concerned about the thing you care about?

Community matters, and we generally come up with better ideas when we work them out in groups. Certainly, we have larger impact when we motivate each other and work together. Remember, it's movements that make big changes, not heroes that fix things for us.

Where are your people? Where will you find them?

Choose:

What is one small thing you can do this week?

If you have found or gathered your community of cause, this may be a good question to bring to them. If you have not yet done that, maybe this step will have something to do with finding or convening them.

- How can you step toward this thing you care about in some small way? What's one small thing you can do right now, or at the latest, in the next two weeks?

Note that I said *small* (perhaps I should write *SMALL* in great big letters, with full irony intended). This isn't about being a hero. It's about getting started and moving in the right direction.

Commit:

Write it down, then do that thing.

Really.

Write it on a piece of paper right now and put that piece of paper on your bathroom mirror, or in your pocket, or on your dashboard, or in your purse, or wherever it is going to nudge you until you get it done.

When you do it, you can put that piece of paper on your fridge in celebration, or burn it with a prayer of thanksgiving, or just recycle it.

Rinse and Repeat:

Yeah, I know. That's not a question (and it doesn't even start with *C*!).

Taking that first step is wonderful and huge. You've just taken a step from being passive to being an active-ist. You're engaging with something you care about, and this is, in fact, how the world changes.

This is not the end of the story, however; it's the beginning. When you're done, there are a few more questions that come up:

- What did you learn from that experience?

- What will you do now?

- Does your experience call you further into commitment to that issue, or are you feeling pulled elsewhere?

As soon as you're ready, go back to question one and do it again.

Blessings on the journey that unfolds.

CONCLUSION

The news is heavy today as I write. Yet another mass shooting, a war in Ukraine, not to mention less-publicized wars in Yemen, Ethiopia, Eritrea, and Afghanistan, and other places, state violence at a funeral in Palestine, Muslims under attack in India, COVID-19 case numbers rising once more, etc. Hope can be hard to come by, and almost everyone I love seems to be carrying the weight of such events.

What do we do with all of this violence, need, oppression, and injustice? How do we respond and not succumb to despair? And what do we do with our deep grief and rage? Answers to those questions are not simple, of course, and I certainly don't have all of them.

What I can offer is this: Action can be healing, both to our own sense of inadequacy and to the world around us.

The global pandemic that disrupted nearly everything in the last few years invited us into new ways to think about our lives and what matters to us. Conversations that began with wistful nostalgia and a hope to "return to normal" seemed gradually to give way to the acknowledgment that the old normal wasn't working very well for many people. Many of us seemed to realize that rather than going back, we could go forward to a better way of being in relationship with each other. I have seen that happen in certain pockets of community, and I remain hopeful that there is potential for new ways to create and practice a healthier society.

If we are going to do that, though, it will take many of us. I hope this book has been helpful to you in thinking about what might be yours to do.

Discern what is yours in this moment—not what you are called to do with your life, but what small thing you are called to do next. Do it. And then do the next right thing. This is the shape and the pace of change.

Find your people. If you are trying to do this work alone, you are still seduced by the Hero Narrative. It's a lie. Let it go.

If you are set back by your own errors, try again. The world is changed by imperfect people, working in imperfect groups and institutions. Keep coming back.

Rest and care for yourself as part of your discipline. If you are healing the part of the world that is you, you are healing a part of the world.

Nurture the people around you who are also trying to do good work and give them space to shine. Step back sometimes, and encourage them to step forward.

Set achievable goals in community and divide up the work. Then set deadlines to get those things done and meet up again to see what you have learned and what the next steps are.

This is the work, friends. Change comes as an accumulation of many small efforts. Let's do the work that is ours to do.

You do not have to fix the world. You can't.

You do not have to save the world. You can't.

But it is not naive to think you can *change* the world. In fact, you cannot live in the world and *not* change it. Everything you do changes the world, whether you like it or not. And the big changes we so desperately need are, in the end, made up of small ones.

So, which changes will you make?

Endnotes

Preface

p. xviii **"As Lee Reich writes in Fine Gardening magazine…"**

Reich, Lee, *To Stake or Not to Stake.* Taunton's Fine Gardening, Issue 84, 2003. https://www.finegardening.com/article/to-stake-or-not-to-stake

p. xxiv **"In their book *The Dragonfly Effect*…"**

Smith, Andy, and Jennifer Lynn Aaker. *The Dragonfly Effect.* San Francisco, CA: Jossey-Bass, 2010, pp. xiv-xv.

p. xxvi **"Alexia Salvatierra and Peter Heltzel point out…"**

Salvatierra, Alexia, and Peter Heltzel. *Faith-Rooted Organizing: Mobilizing the Church in Service to the World.* Downers Grove, IL: InterVarsity Press, 2014, p. 88

Chapter 1: Changing My World

p. 11 **"Historian Howard Zinn argues…"**

Zinn, Howard. *A People's History of the United States.* New York, NY: HarperCollins Publishers, 2005, p. 8.

Chapter 2: What Are You Talking About?

p. 13 **"The German philosopher Johann Georg Hamann…"**

Koestler, Arthur. *The Act of Creation.* New York: Penguin Books, 1990, p. 173.

p. 14 **"'Hope is not prognostication…'"**

Havel, Václav. *Disturbing the Peace.* Translated by Paul Wilson. New York: Vintage Books, [1986] 1991, p. 181-182.

p. 17 **"what the political theorist Carl Boggs called *prefigurative movements*"**

Engler, Paul and Mark Engler, *This Is An Uprising.* New York: Nation Books, 2016.

p. 17   **"Beckerman quotes Mahmoud Salem, one of the Tahrir revolutionaries..."**

Beckerman, Gal. *The Quiet Before: On the Unexpected Origins of Radical Ideas.* New York: Crown, an imprint of Random House, a division of Penguin Random House, LLC, 2022, p. 178.

p. 14   **"The historian Howard Zinn writes..."**

Zinn, Howard. *A Power Governments Cannot Suppress.* San Francisco, CA: City Lights Publishers, 2006, p. 270.

p. 16   **"Since 1976, Habitat for Humanity..."**

https://www.habitat.org/stories/what-is-sweat-equity

p. 16   **"Abraham Jam, a musical trio..."** https://abrahamjam.com

p. 19   **"In his 2012 book *Across that Bridge*, Lewis described..."**

Lewis, John. *Across that Bridge.* New York: Hyperion, 2012, 153.

p. 25   **"...positive peace and negative peace..."**

Galtung, Johan. *An Editorial.* Journal of Peace Research, 1964. p. 25 https://journals.sagepub.com/doi/pdf/10.1177/002234336400100101

p. 26   **"...we have to make 'good trouble'..."**

Reeves, Jay. *John Lewis' legacy shaped in 1965 on 'Bloody Sunday'* AP News. July 18, 2020 https://apnews.com/article/us-news-ap-top-news-voting-selma-voting-rights-eda3ffe8fbfcf7727270e67bba1c9566

p. 29   **"Mediation is demonstrably better at resolving..."**

Chris Guthrie and James Levine, A "Party Satisfaction" Perspective on a Comprehensive Mediation Statute, 13 Ohio State Journal on Dispute Resolution. 885 (1998) Available at: https://scholarship.law.vanderbilt.edu/faculty-publications/708

Chapter 4: Out of the Blue

p. 43   **"...John Lewis did not start out being beaten into a coma..."**

Lewis, John. *Walking with the Wind.* New York: Harvest Books,1999, pp. 75–87.

Chapter 5: Heroes and Movements

p. 48   **"Mrs. Parks had Native American and White ancestry as well."**

Brinkley, Douglas. *Rosa Parks: A Life.* New York: Viking Penguin, 2000, pp. 15-18.

p. 48   **"That is exactly what happened on December 1, 1955."**

Parks, Rosa. *My Story.* New York: Scholastic, 1992, pp. 77, 110-116.

p. 52   **"Paul Loeb articulates this well in his bestseller *Soul of a Citizen*..."**

Loeb, Paul. *Soul of a Citizen.* New York: St. Martin's Press, 1999, p. 34.

p. 53   **"...famed Catholic Worker activist Dorothy Day ..."**

Van Biema, David. "Rhythm of the Saints: Candidate Saints: Dorothy Day." *Time Magazine.* http://content.time.com/time/specials/packages/article/0,28804,1850894_1850895_1850863,00.html.

p. 53   **"James Martin, S.J., further quoted her as saying..."**

Martin, James, S.J. "Don't Call Me A Saint?" *America: The Jesuit Review.*

https://www.americamagazine.org/content/all-things/dont-call-me-saint

p. 53   **"In an interview with the *New York Times*, Wesley Autry said..."**

Buckley, Cara. "Man Is Rescued by Stranger on Subway Tracks." *The New York Times,* January 3, 2007.

p. 53   **"In George W. Bush's 2007 State of the Union Address..."**

The White House. "President Bush Delivers State of the Union Address." January 23, 2007. http://georgewbush-whitehouse.archives.gov/news/releases/2007/01/20070123-2.html.

p. 54   **"Ava DuVernay fought to rewrite the script..."**
Galloway, Stephen. "Ava DuVernay Wishes She'd Challenged
"Privileged, Pedestrian" Criticism of 'Selma'". *The
Hollywood Reporter,* March 7, 2018.

https://www.hollywoodreporter.com/news/general-
news/ava-duvernay-wishes-shed-challenged-privileged-
pedestrian-criticism-selma-1092379/

p. 57   **"It was called 'The 8 Most Overrated People in
History'..."**
Juddery, Mark. "The 8 Most Overrated People in
History." *The Huffington Post,* August 21, 2010. http://
www.huffingtonpost.com/mark-juddery/overrated-
people_b_688237.html#s129491&title=Mahatma_Gandhi.

p. 59   **"By 1955, 64 percent of U.S. households had
televisions."**
Cokeley, Grant. "Number of TV Households in America:
1950-1978." *The American Century.*
https://americancentury.omeka.wlu.edu/items/
show/136.

p. 59   **"Rosa Parks seemed to agree..."**
Brook, Tom Vanden. "Parks' courage changed nation." *USA
Today,* October 25, 2005.
http://usatoday30.usatoday.com/news/nation/2005-10-
24-parks-detailedobit_x.htm.

p. 60   **"Between 2000 and 2006 alone, organized nonviolent
civilian movements..."**
Stephan, Maria J., and Erica Chenoweth. "Why Civil
Resistance Works: The Strategic Logic of Nonviolent
Conflict." *International Security*, vol. 33, no. 1, 2008, pp.
7–44. *JSTOR*, http://www.jstor.org/stable/40207100.
Accessed 25 Aug. 2022.

p. 60   **"Étienne de la Boétie, a young sixteenth-century
political theorist..."**
Boétie, Etienne. The Discourse of Voluntary Servitude.
Unknown, 1576. Online Library of Liberty, https://oll.
libertyfund.org/title/kurz-the-discourse-of-voluntary-
servitude.

p. 60   **"And movements don't need lots of leaders; they need lots of participants..."**
One of my favorite illustrations of this concept is a video by Derek Sivers: http://sivers.org/ff

Chapter 6: Small Change

p. 61   **"as Rosa Parks wrote in her autobiography..."**
Parks, Rosa. *My Story*. New York: Scholastic, 1992, p. 136

p. 62   **"I was the only woman there..."**
Parks, Rosa. *My Story*. New York: Scholastic, 1992, p. 81

p. 67   **"...one of my favorites is the story of Jo Ann Robinson..."**
Robinson, Jo Ann Gibson. *The Montgomery Bus Boycott and the Women Who Started It*. Knoxville: The University of Tennessee Press, 1987, pp. 50–54.

Chapter 7: The Flawed Hero

p. 74   **"Aleksandr Solzhenitsyn got it right when he said..."**
Solzhenitsyn, Aleksandr. *The Gulag Archipelago 1918–56*. Translated by Thomas P. Whitney. New York: Harper & Row, 1973.

Chapter 8: Paved with Good Intentions

p. 78   **"Healthcare activist, doctor, and author Paul Farmer has said..."**
Farmer, Paul. Partners in Health Website. http://www.pih.org/.

p. 80   **"The books *Toxic Charity* and *When Helping Hurts*..."**
Lupton, Robert D. *Toxic Charity*. New York: HarperOne, 2012.

Corbett, Steve, and Brian Fikkert. *When Helping Hurts*. Chicago: Moody Publishers, 2012.

p. 83   **"Between 1960 and 1980, the number of personal-service businesses..."**
National Research Council. America Becoming: Racial Trends and Their Consequences: Volume II. Washington,

DC: The National Academies Press. 2001. p. 190. https://doi.org/10.17226/9719.

p. 83   **"...more than 38,000 black teachers lost their jobs after the Brown v. Board of Education ruling."**

Oakley, Deirdre, Stowell, Jacob & Logan, John R. "The Impact of Desegregation on Black Teachers in the Metropolis, 1970-2000," Ethnic and Racial Studies 39, no. 9 (2009): 1576-1598.

Chapter 9: Movement in the Wrong Direction

p. 87   **"In chapter one he wrote..."**

Alinsky, Saul. *Rules for Radicals: A Practical Primer for Realistic Radicals*. New York: Random House, 1971. p.3.

p. 87   **"Then-President Trump's response to these demonstrations..."**

Choi, Matthew. "Trump claims 'paid protesters' during Kavanaugh confirmation 'haven't gotten their checks'". *Politico*. October 9, 2018.

https://www.politico.com/story/2018/10/09/trump-kavanaugh-paid-protesters-883617

p. 88   **"As Sharyl Attkison wrote in her book *The Smear*..."**

Atkisson, Sharyl. *The Smear: How Shady Political Operatives and Fake News Control What You See, What You Think, and How You Vote*. New York, NY: Harper, 2017. p. 120.

p. 89   **"As reported in New Orleans' *The Lens*..."**

Stein, Michael Isaac. "Entergy acknowledges astroturfing campaign for power plant, but says it didn't know about it." *The Lens*. May 10, 2018. https://thelensnola.org/2018/05/10/entergy-says-a-public-relations-firm-hired-people-to-speak-on-behalf-of-its-new-power-plant/

p. 89   **Each hired attendee was paid $60, and those with speaking roles were paid $200.**
Stein, Michael Isaac. "Documents detail price, logistics behind the campaign to pay actors to support New Orleans power plant." *The Lens*. June 13, 2018.
https://thelensnola.org/2018/06/13/entergy-spent-55000-on-an-astroturfing-campaign-for-a-new-power-plant-in-new-orleans/

p. 89   **"in February of 2019, the City Council voted unanimously to let ..."**

Dermansky, Julie. "Entergy Poised to Get Green Light for Gas Plant Despite Role in Paying Actors." *DeSmog*. Feb. 19, 2019.

p. 90   **"As Leo Gertner and Moshe Marvit wrote in the *Washington Post*..."**

Gertner, Leo, and Marvit, Moshe. "So What if protesters are paid?" *Washington Post*. April 26, 2017.

p. 91   **"As political comic John Oliver argues..."**

Oliver, John. *Astroturfing: Last Week Tonight with John Oliver*. HBO. August 13, 2018.
https://youtu.be/Fmh4RdIwswE
Note that this video contains raunchy humor, and may not be appropriate for all audiences.

p. 92   **"Austin Kessler, who pulled the parade permit for that event..."**
Beckerman, Gal. *The Quiet Before: On the Unexpected Origins of Radical Ideas*. New York: Crown, an imprint of Random House, a division of Penguin Random House, LLC, 2022, p. 190, 204.

p. 91   **"Professor Stanley S. Taylor writes..."**

Taylor, Stanley S. "Why American boys join street gangs." *International Journal of Sociology and Anthropology*. December, 2013. https://academicjournals.org/article/article1382351514_Taylor.pdf

p. 92   **"In the Southern Poverty Law Center's 2021 compilation of statistics..."**

Southern Poverty Law Center. "Ku Klux Klan". SPLC, 2022. P. 44

p. 95   **"In her popular TED talk, Megan Phelps-Roper..."**

Phelps-Roper, Megan. "I grew up in the Westboro Baptist Church. Here's why I left." TED.com. March 6, 2017. https://www.ted.com/talks/megan_phelps_roper_i_grew_up_in_the_westboro_baptist_church_here_s_why_i_left?utm_campaign=tedspread&utm_medium=referral&utm_source=tedcomshare

Chapter 10: Community

p. 97   **"As clown activist Patch Adams writes in his book**
           House Calls..."

Adams, Patch, M.D. *House Calls: How We Can All Heal the
World One Visit at a Time.* San Francisco, CA: Robert D.
Reed Publishers, 1998, p. 44.

p. 98   **"As sociologist John Brueggemann writes in his book**
           Rich, Free, and Miserable..."

Brueggemann, John. *Rich, Free, and Miserable.* New York:
Rowman and Littlefield Publishers, 2012, p. 105.

p. 101   **"He chose to humanize his oppressor..."**

Nolen, Stephanie. "Mandela's miraculous capacity for
forgiveness a carefully calibrated strategy." *The Globe and
Mail*, December 5. 2013
https://www.theglobeandmail.com/news/world/nelson-
mandela/mandelas-miraculous-capacity-for-forgiveness-a-
carefully-calibrated-strategy/article548192/

p. 103   **"In the months following the 9/11 attacks, my friend
           Lyndon Harris..."**

For more on that story, I recommend Krystyna Sanderson's
photo book, *Light at Ground Zero* (Baltimore, MD: Square
Halo Books, 2004).

p. 109   **"As Roger Fisher and William Ury write in their small
           and seminal book..."**

Fisher, Roger, and William Ury. *Getting to Yes: Negotiating
Agreement Without Giving In.* New York: Penguin Books,
1983, p. 42.

p. 113   **"In their insightful book *Switch: How to Change Things
           When Change Is Hard...*"**

Heath, Chip, and Dan Heath. *Switch: How to Change Things
When Change Is Hard.* New York: Broadway Books, 2010, p.
222.

p.118   **"... dramatic stories told by Rev. Barber and Rev. Kojo
           Nantambu..."**

For more on the Wilmington Ten, see: http://www2.lib.
unc.edu/ncc/ref/nchistory/feb2005/

Chapter 11: Creativity

p. 123 **"On May 26, 2007, the Ku Klux Klan gathered for a rally..."**

Santoso, Alex. "Clowns Kicked KKK Asses." *Neatorama*, September 3, 2007. http://www.neatorama. com/2007/09/03/clowns-kicked-kkk-asses/#!bn4liE.

p. 123 **"The problem with the first approach is that, in the words of Dr. King..."**

King, Martin Luther Jr. "Loving Your Enemies." *Strength to Love*. Minneapolis, MN: Fortress Press, [1963] 2010, p. 47.

p. 124 **"...Martin Luther King, Jr. wrote in his famous 'Letter from a Birmingham Jail.'"**

King, Martin Luther, Jr. "Letter from a Birmingham Jail." April 16, 1963. Philadelphia: University of Pennsylvania African Studies Center. http://www.africa.upenn.edu/ Articles_Gen/Letter_Birmingham.html.

p. 127 **"As John Lewis wrote in his book *Across that Bridge*..."**

Lewis, John. *Across that Bridge*. Hyperion: New York, NY, 2012, p. 136.

p. 127 **"As reported in the Guardian..."**

https://www.theguardian.com/world/2014/nov/18/neo-nazis-tricked-into-raising-10000-for-charity

p. 127 **"Artist Peter von Tiesenhausen was being threatened by oil corporations..."**

"Opposition to Drilling Elevated to an Art Form." *The Edmonton Journal*, February 27, 2006. http://www.canada. com/story_print.html?id=a271ed7f-d512-4a26-9b32-226ba7bfb1ea&sponsor=.

p. 128 **"Julia Cameron, in her classic book on creativity, *The Artist's Way*, writes..."**

Cameron, Julia. *The Artist's Way*. New York: Tarcher/Putnam, 1992, p. 3.

p. 130 **"Rosa Parks, at the end of her autobiography...wrote with wonder..."**

Parks, Rosa. *My Story*. New York: Puffin Books, 1992, p. 186.

p. 131   **"Thoreau describes these two steps to creation…"**

Thoreau, Henry David. *Walden.* New York: Bantam Books, [1854] 1989, p. 343.

p. 131   **"Emily Dickinson said it another way…"**

Grabher, Gurdun, Roland Hagenbuchle, and Cristanne Miller, eds. *The Emily Dickinson Handbook.* Amherst: University of Massachusetts Press, 1998, p. 282.

p. 132   **"The respected conflict transformation theorist and practitioner John Paul Lederach…"**

Lederach, John Paul. *The Moral Imagination.* Oxford: Oxford University Press, 2005, p. 69.

p. 133   **"The famed Russian actor and theater director, Konstantin Sergeievich Stanislavski…"**

White, R. Andrew, ed. *The Routledge Companion to Stanislovsky.* New York: Routledge, 2014.

p. 133   **"Kim Rosen, the author of *Saved By a Poem*…writes that…"**

Rosen, Kim. "Where Words Melt Walls: The Peacemaking Power of Poetry." *The Huffington Post,* June 21, 2010. http://www.huffingtonpost.com/kim-rosen/where-words-melt-walls-th_b_615133.html.

p. 134   **"In another effort to approach a serious topic through art, I put the story of the clowns and the Klan to rhyme…"**

LaMotte, David. Black Mountain, NC: Dryad Publishing, Inc. *White Flour.* 2012. www.whiteflourbook.com

p. 134   **"it was listed by Essence magazine…"**

Essence. "11 Books to Teach Your Kids About Racism and Discrimination." *Essence.* Dec. 6, 2020. https://www.essence.com/entertainment/childrens-books-racism/

p. 134   **"In November of 2012, there was a neo-Nazi rally in Charlotte, NC…"**

Manual-Logan, Ruth. "KKK Protestors Clowned by Counter-Protest, Outnumbered 5 to 1." *News One,* November 13, 2012. http://newsone.com/2081264/kkk-charlotte-nc/.

Chapter 12: Stumbling toward the Light

p. 149 **"In her fascinating Book *Being Wrong*, Kathryn Schulz writes…"**

Schulz, Kathryn. *Being Wrong: Adventures in the Margin of Error.* New York: HarperCollins, 2010.

Chapter 14: What's Most Important?

p. 157 **"…given that the average person in the U.S. now has several careers…"**

Morrison, Robert F., and Jerome Adams. *Contemporary Career Development Issues.* Hillsdale, NJ: Lawrence Erblaum Associates, 1991, p. 80.

p. 159 **"Noam Chomsky, the famous linguist and activist, talking with Bill Moyers…"**

Moyers, Bill. *A World of Ideas.* New York: Doubleday, 1989, p. 56.

p. 159 **"'Compassion fatigue' is well documented."**

"Self-Study Unit 3: Photography and Trauma." *The Dart Center for Journalism and Trauma.* Columbia University Graduate School of Journalism. http://dartcenter.org/content/self-study-unit-3-photography-trauma-3#. U9Y6d4BdWGl.

Chapter 15: What's Bugging You?

p. 169 **"According to theologian and author Gil Bailie…"**

Bailie, Gil. *Violence Unveiled.* New York: Crossroad Publishing Company, 1996, p. xv.

p. 171 **"'Faith contains a certain ferocity…'"**

Levoy, Gregg Michael. *Callings: Finding and Following an Authentic Life.* New York: Three Rivers Press, 1997, p. 265.

p. 176 **"In the last few pages of Rosa Parks' autobiography…"**

Parks, Rosa. *My Story.* New York: Puffin Books, 1992, p. 180.

Chapter 17: Personal Sustainability

p. 180   **"Alexis Ohanian, the co-founder of Reddit..."**

Togoh, Isabel. "Michael Seibel Becomes Reddit's First Black Board Member After Alexis Ohanian's Resignation." Forbes. com. June 10, 2020.

https://www.forbes.com/sites/isabeltogoh/2020/06/10/ michael-seibel-becomes-reddits-first-black- board-member-after-alexis-ohanians- resignation/?sh=3f9ea54d430a

Chapter 18: The Power In Who You Are

p. 185   **"Ivo Markovic, the founder of the choir, tells the story of its origins..."**

Conrad, Keziah. "Ivo Markovich." *The Beyond Intractability Project.* Boulder: Conflict Information Consortium of the University of Colorado, March 2007. http://www. beyondintractability.org/profile/ivo-markovic

p. 185   **"In an article about Pontanima, Andrew Packman writes..."**

Packman, Andrew. "Interfaith Repertoire: A Bosnian Choir Sings Reconciliation." *The Christian Century,* June 13. 2012.

p. 186   **"Billionaire Warren Buffet's advocacy for raising taxes on the wealthy..."**

Klebnikov, Sergei. "Billionaire Warren Buffet on Raising Taxes on the Rich: 'I'm Fine with It.'" Money.com. February 25, 2019. https://money.com/buffett-wants-to-tax-rich- more/

p. 187   **"Stephen Colbert ran an ironic segment..."**
Colbert, Stephen. "People Who Are Destroying America: Johnny Cummings." Comedy Central. August 14, 2013.

https://www.cc.com/video/y58ew9/the-colbert-report- people-who-are-destroying-america-johnny-cummings

p. 193   **"The governor called Abby at home one night..."**
Meyer, Erin. "Governor gives Grayslake girl good news on
plastic bag ban." *Chicago Tribune.* August 27, 2012.

https://www.chicagotribune.com/suburbs/ct-xpm-2012-
08-27-ct-met-plastic-bag-bill-veto-20120827-story.html

p. 194   **"...they fall on bell hooks' book *Ain't I a Woman.*"**

hooks, bell. *Ain't I a Woman: Black Women and Feminism.*
New York: South End Press, 1981, pp. 159–60.

Chapter 19: The Not-So-Radical Activist

p. 197   **"Robinson writes that when she entered his office..."**

Robinson, Jo Ann Gibson. *The Montgomery Bus Boycott and
the Women Who Started It.* Knoxville: The University of
Tennessee Press, 1987, p. 48ff.

p. 199   **"'Dr. Trenholm did not participate personally in the
boycott...'"**

Robinson, Jo Ann Gibson. *The Montgomery Bus Boycott and
the Women Who Started It.* Knoxville: The University of
Tennessee Press, 1987, p. 50.

p. 200   **"...the Spectrum of Allies, created by George Lakey..."**
Training for Change. https://www.trainingforchange.org/
training_tools/spectrum-of-allies/